How to Live a Blessed and FABULOUS Life

DAILY DECLARATIONS
for a Blessed and Fabulous Life

ISIOMA ONUEGWUNWOKE

Trilogy Christian Publishers
A Wholly Owned Subsidiary of Trinity Broadcasting Network
2442 Michelle Drive
Tustin, CA 92780

For information, address Trilogy Christian Publishing
Rights Department, 2442 Michelle Drive, Tustin, CA 92780.

10 9 8 7 6 5 4 3 2 1
Library of Congress Cataloging-in-Publication Data is available.
ISBN 979-8-89333-061-8
ISBN 979-8-89333-062-5 (ebook)

Dedication

This book is dedicated to Almighty God the Father with Whom all things are possible, God the Son—Jesus Christ my Lord and savior, and God the Holy Spirit Who helps and inspires me and without Whom I am nothing.

Foreword

In a world filled with constant challenges and uncertainties, the pursuit of a blessed and fabulous life seems like an elusive dream for many. Yet, in the midst of chaos, there lies a timeless truth that has the power to transform our homes, our hearts, and our lives. *How to Live a Blessed and Fabulous Life* is not just a book; it's a guiding light, a source of inspiration, and a roadmap to a life that transcends the ordinary.

This book comes at a crucial time when our homes need to be fortified by the power of the Almighty's spoken Word, in order to quench the fiery darts of the wicked one. In the pages of this book, you will discover daily manna, which is aimed at helping you develop an intentional habit of reading Scripture and meditating on the profound wisdom of the Almighty. As you embark on this journey, you will find that this intentional practice is not merely a routine but a powerful weapon – a spiritual arsenal that equips you to live a victorious life and surmount the daily pressures that threaten to overwhelm us all.

Each daily declaration is a beacon of hope, a nugget of truth, and a reminder that your life is meant to be nothing short of fabulous.

The author, Isioma (Isy), my friend and sister, whom

I have known for over twenty years, is someone with a loving heart. She is deeply rooted in faith and prayer and is someone whom I know the Almighty Father communicates to in thoughts and in dreams.

May this book be more than just words on a page, may it be a companion on your daily journey, a start to a deeper walk with our Lord and savior Yeshua Hamashiach, and a guide to living a life that reflects the abundance of divine blessings. Get a copy for yourself and get a copy for your children too. Let this book help them develop a closer relationship with the Creator of Heaven and Earth.

As you delve into *How to Live a Blessed and Fabulous Life*, may you find not just a book but a lifeline – a lifeline that connects you to the eternal source of all blessings, making each day a step closer to the glorious and fabulous life you were destined to live.

Shalom,

Dr. Amaka Emereole

Acknowledgements

I would like to express my heartfelt gratitude to my dear husband, Sylvester Onuegwunwoke, and our wonderful children, Chimdi Onuegwunwoke, Kamdi Onuegwunwoke, and Zina Onuegwunwoke, for their love, unwavering support, and encouragement over the course of writing this book. I love and appreciate you all tremendously.

I would also like to specially thank the entire team at Trilogy Christian Publishing, the publishing division of Trinity Broadcasting Network (TBN), for their partnership in bringing this book to fruition.

Introduction

Hello! I hope you are doing well. I have a few questions for you. What have you said today? Have you ever thought about your words? Do you take into consideration the words that you speak over your life? Are you aware of the incredible power that lies in your tongue? According to Proverbs 18: 21 (NIV), "The tongue has the power of life and death, and those who love it will eat its fruit."

Based on this scripture, don't you think it is time to intentionally utilize your tongue to speak your way into the blessed life that God has for you?

The anchor scripture for this book is stated in Job 22:28 (AMP) and says, "You will also decide and decree a thing, and it will be established for you; And the light [of God's favor] will shine upon your ways."

A significant time of my life was spent musing on words that were spoken to me and about me, words that I read and words that I thought. Yes, you can think words. I realized that I focused more on the negative words than the positive words, until I had an encounter with the Holy Spirit that changed my perspective on words.

If you are familiar with the Bible, you have probably come across Proverbs 18:21. I love the way it is stated in the Message translation: "Words kill, words give life;

they're either poison or fruit—you choose" (Proverbs 18:21, MSG)

"You choose." Wow! That was an epiphany for me. So, you mean I get to choose between words that can kill or give life? I believe we can agree that fruit is healthy, tastes good, and is more beneficial to the human body and a much better choice for consumption than poison.

As a result of this biblical truth, I became very intentional about words. They had to be life giving, positive, blessings, grace filled, good words before I spoke them, or received them especially. This revelation stirred up an insatiable desire to dig deep into the Word of God. I began to surround myself and immerse myself with the Word of God. I would pray the Word, declare the Word, sing the Word, display scriptures in my home and office. I was obsessed with the Bible and I still am. It is the blueprint for life. The Word of God is life![1]

A few years ago, I was inspired by the Holy Spirit to share Bible-based monthly prayer themes with my family and friends, which I have included in this book. Subsequently, I was inspired by the Holy Spirit again to write Bible-based daily declarations for an entire year to encourage people to engage in frequent declaration of Scripture and ultimately develop a lifestyle of prayer.

This book includes Bible verses and prayers that you

---

1 "The Spirit gives life; the flesh counts for nothing. The words I have spoken to you—they are full of the Spirit and life" (John 6:63, NIV).

can personalize, decree, declare, and pray with on a daily basis. As you decree and declare the Word of God, you will speak the unfailing promises of God and establish the abundant blessings of God over your life, thus causing you to live the blessed and fabulous life that God has planned for you.

Thank you so much for the honor to share my heart for God and His life-giving Word with you. My prayer is that this book will bless you and all that concerns you in extremely remarkable ways.

Table of Contents

Prologue

Declaration of Salvation

As an expression of God's great love for the world, He made His promise of salvation available to everyone at no cost but to believe in His one and only Son – Jesus Christ. The first step to living a blessed and fabulous life is to believe in Jesus Christ and to accept Him as your Lord and Savior. If you have not taken this step, I encourage you to do so by making the simple declaration below:

I believe and declare that Jesus Christ is Lord. I believe in my heart that God raised Him from the dead. Lord, forgive me for all my sins. Today, I accept Jesus Christ into my life as my Lord and Savior.

Congratulations on your salvation! You have made an incredibly life changing and life-giving decision to accept Jesus Christ as your Lord and Savior. Welcome to a new life. You will begin to experience the unlimited love of God in the most profound ways. I am very excited for you and I am very proud of you!

"For God so loved the world that he gave his one and only Son, that whoever believes in him shall not perish but have eternal life." (John 3:16, NIV)

"If you declare with your mouth, 'Jesus is Lord,' and believe in your heart that God raised him from the dead, you will be saved. For it is with your heart that you believe and are justified, and it is with your mouth that you profess your faith and are saved. As Scripture says, 'Anyone who believes in him will never be put to shame.'" (Romans 10:9-11, NIV)

Let there be a display of God's jaw-dropping, astounding power in our lives in Jesus name.

CHAPTER 1

Jaw-dropping January

You answer our prayers with amazing wonders and with awe-inspiring displays of power. You are the righteous God who helps us like a father. Everyone everywhere looks to you, for you are the confidence of all the earth, even to the farthest islands of the sea. What jaw-dropping, astounding power is yours! You are the mountain maker who sets them all in place."
Psalms 65:5-6 TPT

Happy New Year!

Welcome to Jaw-dropping January!

I am excited about the prayer theme for this month. I believe that it is absolutely apt for the start of the new year.

This month, you will be introduced to the wonders of God in the most powerful and amazing ways as recorded in Scriptures.

I love how the scripture for the first day of January paints the picture of the wonderful way that God comes through for us in the form of an answered prayer. It encourages me to pray more, to ask God to do what seems impossible, and to believe God will bless me in fabulous ways.

I encourage you to become creative and audacious as you pray and make bold biblical declarations and watch God do wonders in your life just as He has promised in His Word.

January 1

BIBLE VERSE(S):

Psalm 65:5-6 NLT

"You faithfully answer our prayers with awesome deeds, O God our savior. You are the hope of everyone on earth, even those who sail on distant seas. You formed the mountains by your power and armed yourself with mighty strength."

PRAYER:

Father, in the name of Jesus Christ, I decree and declare that I shall experience Your jaw-dropping power in my life and in all that concerns me. I thank You because You shall answer my prayers with awesome deeds, O God my savior.

DAILY REFLECTION:

Take a moment to reflect on the Bible verse(s) for today and write your thoughts below:

____

____

____

____

____

____

January 2

BIBLE VERSE(S):

Psalm 65:8 NLT

"Those who live at the ends of the earth stand in awe of your wonders. From where the sun rises to where it sets, you inspire shouts of joy."

PRAYER:

Father, in the name of Jesus Christ, I decree and declare that I will stand in awe, startled, and stunned by the signs and wonders of God in my life and in all that concerns me.

DAILY REFLECTION:

Take a moment to reflect on the Bible verse(s) for today and write your thoughts below:

January 3

BIBLE VERSE(S):

Psalm 147:5 NKJV

"Great is our Lord, and mighty in power; His understanding is infinite."

PRAYER:

Father, I bless You, for You are great and mighty in power, with infinite understanding.

DAILY REFLECTION:

Take a moment to reflect on the Bible verse(s) for today and write your thoughts below:

January 4

BIBLE VERSE(S):

Jeremiah 10:12 ESV

"It is he who made the earth by his power, who established the world by his wisdom, and by his understanding stretched out the heavens."

PRAYER:

Father, in the name of Jesus Christ, I ask that You please fill me with Your power, wisdom and understanding, as You made the earth by Your power, established the world by Your wisdom, and by Your understanding stretched out the heavens.

DAILY REFLECTION:

Take a moment to reflect on the Bible verse(s) for today and write your thoughts below:

BIBLE VERSE(S):

Ephesians 3:20-21 ESV

"Now to him who is able to do far more abundantly than all that we ask or think, according to the power at work within us, to him be glory in the church and in Christ Jesus throughout all generations, forever and ever. Amen."

PRAYER:

Father, in the name of Jesus Christ, I ask that You do far more abundantly than all that I ask or think, according to the power at work within me.

DAILY REFLECTION:

Take a moment to reflect on the Bible verse(s) for today and write your thoughts below:

January 6

BIBLE VERSE(S):

Psalm 77:14 NLT

"You are the God of great wonders! You demonstrate your awesome power among the nations."

PRAYER:

Father, in the name of Jesus Christ, I decree and declare that You are the God of great wonders, and You shall do great wonders in my life. Lord, I ask that You demonstrate Your awesome power in my life, just as You demonstrate Your awesome power among the nations, in the name of Jesus Christ.

DAILY REFLECTION:

Take a moment to reflect on the Bible verse(s) for today and write your thoughts below:

January 7

BIBLE VERSE(S):

John 11:4 ESV

"But when Jesus heard it, he said, 'This illness does not lead to death. It is for the glory of God, so that the Son of God may be glorified through it.'"

PRAYER:

Father, in the name of Jesus Christ, I decree and declare that every situation in my life is for the glory of God, so that Jesus Christ, the Son of God, may be glorified through it.

DAILY REFLECTION:

Take a moment to reflect on the Bible verse(s) for today and write your thoughts below:

January 8

BIBLE VERSE(S):

Mark 16:20 NKJV

"And they went out and preached everywhere, the Lord working with them and confirming the word through the accompanying signs. Amen."

PRAYER:

Father, in the name of Jesus Christ, I decree and declare that there shall be accompanying signs as the Word of God is preached.

DAILY REFLECTION:

Take a moment to reflect on the Bible verse(s) for today and write your thoughts below:

January 9

BIBLE VERSE(S):

Acts 14:3 NIV

"So Paul and Barnabas spent considerable time there, speaking boldly for the Lord, who confirmed the message of his grace by enabling them to perform signs and wonders."

PRAYER:

Father, in the name of Jesus Christ, I decree and declare that as I speak boldly for You, You will confirm the message of Your grace by enabling me to perform signs and wonders.

DAILY REFLECTION:

Take a moment to reflect on the Bible verse(s) for today and write your thoughts below:

January 10

BIBLE VERSE(S):

Hebrews 2:4 NLT

"And God confirmed the message by giving signs and wonders and various miracles and gifts of the Holy Spirit whenever he chose."

PRAYER:

Father, in the name of Jesus Christ, I decree and declare that You shall validate my life with signs, astonishing wonders, all kinds of powerful miracles, and by the gifts of the Holy Spirit.

DAILY REFLECTION:

Take a moment to reflect on the Bible verse(s) for today and write your thoughts below:

January 11

BIBLE VERSE(S):

Jeremiah 32:27 NLT

"I am the Lord, the God of all the peoples of the world. Is anything too hard for me?"

PRAYER:

Father, in the name of Jesus Christ, I decree and declare that You are the Lord, the God of all the peoples of the world. There is nothing too hard for You.

DAILY REFLECTION:

Take a moment to reflect on the Bible verse(s) for today and write your thoughts below:

January 12

BIBLE VERSE(S):

Exodus 14:31 MSG

"But the Israelites walked right through the middle of the sea on dry ground, the waters forming a wall to the right and to the left. God delivered Israel that day from the oppression of the Egyptians. And Israel looked at the Egyptian dead, washed up on the shore of the sea, and realized the tremendous power that God brought against the Egyptians. The people were in reverent awe before God and trusted in God and his servant Moses."

The parting of the red sea remains my absolute favorite miracle recorded in the Bible. It leaves me speechless. It is amazing how powerful the Almighty God is. Take a moment and imagine how dramatic the scene would have been. Just imagine you are walking on dry ground with walls of water on either side. Surely, after witnessing such awesome wonder from God, the Israelites gained a deeper understanding of the kind of God they had. A powerful God, a God who could use the elements of creation to fight for them. One who protected them and truly cared for them. A God who delivered them completely, totally, with no Egyptian left to oppress them. Wow! What a powerful God!

PRAYER:

Father, in the name of Jesus Christ, I decree and declare that You shall deliver me from every evil work, just as

You delivered the Israelites and I shall be in reverent awe before You.

DAILY REFLECTION:

Take a moment to reflect on the Bible verse(s) for today and write your thoughts below:

January 13

BIBLE VERSE(S):

Acts 2:22 NLT

"People of Israel, listen! God publicly endorsed Jesus the Nazarene[a] by doing powerful miracles, wonders, and signs through him, as you well know."

PRAYER:

Father, in the name of Jesus Christ, I ask that You publicly endorse me by doing powerful miracles, wonders, and signs through me.

DAILY REFLECTION:

Take a moment to reflect on the Bible verse(s) for today and write your thoughts below:

January 14

BIBLE VERSE(S):

Psalm 105:5 NKJV

"Remember His marvelous works which He has done, His wonders, and the judgments of His mouth,"

PRAYER:

Father, in the name of Jesus Christ, I decree and declare that I shall remember Your marvelous works and wonders which You have done.

DAILY REFLECTION:

Take a moment to reflect on the Bible verse(s) for today and write your thoughts below:

January 15

BIBLE VERSE(S):

Daniel 3:29-30 ESV

"Therefore I make a decree: Any people, nation, or language that speaks anything against the God of Shadrach, Meshach, and Abednego shall be torn limb from limb, and their houses laid in ruins, for there is no other god who is able to rescue in this way. Then the king promoted Shadrach, Meshach, and Abednego in the province of Babylon."

PRAYER:

Father, in the name of Jesus Christ, I thank You for there is no other God who is able to rescue me in the most powerful way.

DAILY REFLECTION:

Take a moment to reflect on the Bible verse(s) for today and write your thoughts below:

January 16

BIBLE VERSE(S):

Exodus 14:25 ESV

"clogging[a] their chariot wheels so that they drove heavily. And the Egyptians said, "Let us flee from before Israel, for the Lord fights for them against the Egyptians."

PRAYER:

Father, in the name of Jesus Christ, I decree and declare that my enemies shall flee from before me, for the Lord fights for me against them.

DAILY REFLECTION:

Take a moment to reflect on the Bible verse(s) for today and write your thoughts below:

BIBLE VERSE(S):

Deuteronomy 10:21 NIV

"He is the one you praise; he is your God, who performed for you those great and awesome wonders you saw with your own eyes."

PRAYER:

Father, today my heart is full of gratitude for who You are. I praise and thank You, Lord, for being my God and for performing great and awesome wonders that I have seen with my own eyes. I am blessed!

DAILY REFLECTION:

Take a moment to reflect on the Bible verse(s) for today and write your thoughts below:

January 18

BIBLE VERSE(S):

Psalm 139:14 NIV

"I praise you because I am fearfully and wonderfully made; your works are wonderful, I know that full well."

PRAYER:

Father, in the name of Jesus Christ, I praise You that I am fearfully and wonderfully made. I decree and declare that Your works are wonderful—I know that full well.

DAILY REFLECTION:

Take a moment to reflect on the Bible verse(s) for today and write your thoughts below:

January 19

BIBLE VERSE(S):

John 14:12 NKJV

"Most assuredly, I say to you, he who believes in Me, the works that I do he will do also; and greater works than these he will do, because I go to My Father."

PRAYER:

I decree and declare that because I believe in Jesus Christ, the works that He did, I will do also, and greater works than these I will do.

DAILY REFLECTION:

Take a moment to reflect on the Bible verse(s) for today and write your thoughts below:

BIBLE VERSE(S):

Matthew 17:20 ESV

"He said to them, 'Because of your little faith. For truly, I say to you, if you have faith like a grain of mustard seed, you will say to this mountain, "Move from here to there," and it will move, and nothing will be impossible for you.'"

PRAYER:

Father, in the name of Jesus Christ, I decree and declare that with faith, I shall move mountains from here to there and nothing will be impossible for me.

DAILY REFLECTION:

Take a moment to reflect on the Bible verse(s) for today and write your thoughts below:

January 21

BIBLE VERSE(S):

Revelation 21:4 NLT

"He will wipe every tear from their eyes, and there will be no more death or sorrow or crying or pain. All these things are gone forever."

PRAYER:

Father, in the name of Jesus Christ, I thank You for wiping every tear from my eyes.

DAILY REFLECTION:

Take a moment to reflect on the Bible verse(s) for today and write your thoughts below:

January 22

BIBLE VERSE(S):

Hebrews 4:12 NIV

"For the word of God is alive and active. Sharper than any double-edged sword, it penetrates even to dividing soul and spirit, joints and marrow; it judges the thoughts and attitudes of the heart."

PRAYER:

Father, in the name of Jesus Christ, I decree and declare that the Word of God is alive and active.

DAILY REFLECTION:

Take a moment to reflect on the Bible verse(s) for today and write your thoughts below:

January 23

BIBLE VERSE(S):

Ephesians 3:20-21 NKJV

"Now to Him who is able to do exceedingly abundantly above all that we ask or think, according to the power that works in us, to Him be glory in the church by Christ Jesus to all generations, forever and ever. Amen."

PRAYER:

Father, in the name of Jesus Christ, I decree and declare that You will do exceedingly and abundantly above all that I ask or think, and all the glory shall be to You, forever and ever.

DAILY REFLECTION:

Take a moment to reflect on the Bible verse(s) for today and write your thoughts below:

January 24

BIBLE VERSE(S):

Acts 4:30 NLT

"Stretch out your hand with healing power; may miraculous signs and wonders be done through the name of your holy servant Jesus."

PRAYER:

Father, in the name of Jesus Christ, I decree and declare that as I stretch out my hand with healing power; may miraculous signs and wonders be done through the name of Jesus Christ.

DAILY REFLECTION:

Take a moment to reflect on the Bible verse(s) for today and write your thoughts below:

January 25

BIBLE VERSE(S):

Mark 16:17-18 NLT

"These miraculous signs will accompany those who believe: They will cast out demons in my name, and they will speak in new languages. They will be able to handle snakes with safety, and if they drink anything poisonous, it won't hurt them. They will be able to place their hands on the sick, and they will be healed."

PRAYER:

Father, in the name of Jesus Christ, I decree and declare that miraculous signs will accompany me because I believe.

DAILY REFLECTION:

Take a moment to reflect on the Bible verse(s) for today and write your thoughts below:

January 26

BIBLE VERSE(S):

Acts 4:31 MSG

"While they were praying, the place where they were meeting trembled and shook. They were all filled with the Holy Spirit and continued to speak God's Word with fearless confidence."

PRAYER:

Father, in the name of Jesus Christ, I ask that You fill me with the Holy Spirit, and I will continue to speak God's Word with fearless confidence.

DAILY REFLECTION:

Take a moment to reflect on the Bible verse(s) for today and write your thoughts below:

January 27

BIBLE VERSE(S):

John 16:13 NLT

"When the Spirit of truth comes, he will guide you into all truth. He will not speak on his own but will tell you what he has heard. He will tell you about the future."

PRAYER:

Father, in the name of Jesus Christ, I decree and declare that the Spirit of truth guides me into all truth, telling me what He has heard and telling me about the future.

DAILY REFLECTION:

Take a moment to reflect on the Bible verse(s) for today and write your thoughts below:

January 28

BIBLE VERSE(S):

John 5:19-23 MSG

"So Jesus explained himself at length. 'I'm telling you this straight. The Son can't independently do a thing, only what he sees the Father doing. What the Father does, the Son does. The Father loves the Son and includes him in everything he is doing.

But you haven't seen the half of it yet, for in the same way that the Father raises the dead and creates life, so does the Son. The Son gives life to anyone he chooses. Neither he nor the Father shuts anyone out. The Father handed all authority to judge over to the Son so that the Son will be honored equally with the Father. Anyone who dishonors the Son, dishonors the Father, for it was the Father's decision to put the Son in the place of honor.'"

PRAYER:

Father, in the name of Jesus Christ, I thank You for loving me and including me in everything You are doing, just as you did with Your Son, Jesus.

DAILY REFLECTION:

Take a moment to reflect on the Bible verse(s) for today and write your thoughts below:

January 29

BIBLE VERSE(S):

Exodus 14:14 AMP

"The Lord will fight for you while you [only need to] keep silent and remain calm."

PRAYER:

Father, in the name of Jesus Christ, I decree and declare that You will fight for me while I only need to keep silent and remain calm.

DAILY REFLECTION:

Take a moment to reflect on the Bible verse(s) for today and write your thoughts below:

BIBLE VERSE(S):

2 Peter 1:3 NLT

"By his divine power, God has given us everything we need for living a godly life. We have received all of this by coming to know him, the one who called us to himself by means of his marvelous glory and excellence."

PRAYER:

Father, in the name of Jesus Christ, I decree and declare that You have given me everything I need to live a godly life by Your divine power.

DAILY REFLECTION:

Take a moment to reflect on the Bible verse(s) for today and write your thoughts below:

January 31

BIBLE VERSE(S):

1 Chronicles 29:11 NLT

"Yours, O Lord, is the greatness, the power, the glory, the victory, and the majesty. Everything in the heavens and on earth is yours, O Lord, and this is your kingdom. We adore you as the one who is over all things."

PRAYER:

Father, in the name of Jesus Christ, I decree and declare that Yours, O Lord, is the greatness, the power, the glory, the victory, and the majesty.

DAILY REFLECTION:

Take a moment to reflect on the Bible verse(s) for today and write your thoughts below:

Father, let Your favor surround us in the month of February and beyond in Jesus name.

CHAPTER 2

Favorable February

For You, O Lord will bless the righteous; with favor You will surround him as with a shield."
Psalm 5:12 NKJV

Welcome to Favorable February!

I love the subject of God's favor. For me, the favor of God is a reminder of God's power and ability to indulge His children beyond the norm.

Anytime I experience the favor of God, it feels like an extra blessing with His signature, letting me know without a shadow of doubt that He did it.

The favor of God is palpable, it is distinctive, it is captivating, and extremely pleasant.

I encourage you to pray for God's favor every single day, even beyond the month of February. It will make an undeniable difference in your life.

February 1

BIBLE VERSE(S):

Isaiah 61:1-3 NIV

"The Year of the Lord's Favor: The Spirit of the Sovereign Lord is on me, because the Lord has anointed me to proclaim good news to the poor. He has sent me to bind up the brokenhearted, to proclaim freedom for the captives and release from darkness for the prisoners, to proclaim the year of the Lord's favor and the day of vengeance of our God, to comfort all who mourn, and provide for those who grieve in Zion— to bestow on them a crown of beauty instead of ashes, the oil of joy instead of mourning, and a garment of praise instead of a spirit of despair. They will be called oaks of righteousness, a planting of the Lord for the display of his splendor."

PRAYER:

Father, in the name of Jesus Christ, I decree and declare that this is the year of Your favor. I shall be called an oak of righteousness, a planting of the Lord for the display of His splendor.

DAILY REFLECTION:

Take a moment to reflect on the Bible verse(s) for today and write your thoughts below:

BIBLE VERSE(S):

Psalm 30:5 NKJV

"For His anger is but for a moment, His favor is for life; Weeping may endure for a night, But joy comes in the morning.'

PRAYER:

Father, in the name of Jesus Christ, I thank You for a lifetime of Your favor. Thank You for the assurance of joy that comes in the morning. I receive Your favor for life. Let Your favor be evident in all that concerns me, in the mighty name of Jesus Christ.

DAILY REFLECTION:

Take a moment to reflect on the Bible verse(s) for today and write your thoughts below:

February 3

BIBLE VERSE(S):

Psalm 40:13 NIV

"Be pleased to save me, Lord; come quickly, Lord, to help me."

PRAYER:

Father, in the name of Jesus Christ, I ask that You favor me and be pleased to save and deliver me. Lord, I ask that You come quickly to help me today and all the days of my life in the mighty name of Jesus Christ.

DAILY REFLECTION:

Take a moment to reflect on the Bible verse(s) for today and write your thoughts below:

BIBLE VERSE(S):

Psalm 69:13 NIV

"But I pray to you, Lord, in the time of your favor; in your great love, O God, answer me with your sure salvation."

PRAYER:

Father, in the name of Jesus Christ, I decree and declare that in the time of your favor; in your great love, You will answer me with Your sure salvation.

DAILY REFLECTION:

Take a moment to reflect on the Bible verse(s) for today and write your thoughts below:

BIBLE VERSE(S):

Proverbs 16:15 NLT

"When the king smiles, there is life; his favor refreshes like a spring rain."

PRAYER:

Father, in the name of Jesus Christ, I decree and declare that Your favor will refresh me like a spring rain. Thank You, Lord, for a rain of Your favor upon my life.

DAILY REFLECTION:

Take a moment to reflect on the Bible verse(s) for today and write your thoughts below:

BIBLE VERSE(S):

Psalm 84:11 AMP

"For the Lord God is a sun and shield; The Lord bestows grace and favor and honor; No good thing will He withhold from those who walk uprightly."

PRAYER:

Father, in the name of Jesus Christ, I decree and declare that You are a sun and shield. Lord God, I thank You for bestowing grace and favor and honor on me.

DAILY REFLECTION:

Take a moment to reflect on the Bible verse(s) for today and write your thoughts below:

BIBLE VERSE(S):

Genesis 6:8 AMP

"But Noah found favor and grace in the eyes of the Lord."

PRAYER:

Father, in the name of Jesus Christ, I ask that as Noah found favor and grace in the eyes of the Lord, I shall also find favor and grace in Your eyes Lord.

DAILY REFLECTION:

Take a moment to reflect on the Bible verse(s) for today and write your thoughts below:

BIBLE VERSE(S):

Luke 1:30 NLT

"'Don't be afraid, Mary,' the angel told her, 'for you have found favor with God!'"

PRAYER:

Father, in the name of Jesus Christ, today as I ask that I shall find favor with You, my Lord and God.

PRAYER:

Father, in the name of Jesus Christ, I thank You for Your supernatural provision and abundant supply of all my needs and wants. I declare that according to Psalm 78:26-27, I shall not lack and Your heavenly winds of miracle power will constantly blow in my favor, in the name of Jesus Christ.

DAILY REFLECTION:

Take a moment to reflect on the Bible verse(s) for today and write your thoughts below:

February 9

BIBLE VERSE(S):

Genesis 12:2 ESV

"And I will make of you a great nation, and I will bless you and make your name great, so that you will be a blessing."

PRAYER:

Father, in the name of Jesus Christ, I decree and declare that You shall make of me a great nation, and You will bless me with abundant increase of favors and make my name great so that I will be a blessing.

DAILY REFLECTION:

Take a moment to reflect on the Bible verse(s) for today and write your thoughts below:

BIBLE VERSE(S):

Isaiah 60:10 AMP

"Foreigners will build up your walls, And their kings will serve you; For in My [righteous] wrath I struck you, But in My favor and grace I have had compassion on you."

PRAYER:

Father, in the name of Jesus Christ, I decree and declare that in Your favor and grace You will continue to have compassion on me.

DAILY REFLECTION:

Take a moment to reflect on the Bible verse(s) for today and write your thoughts below:

February 11

BIBLE VERSE(S):

Judges 6:17 NIV

"Gideon replied, 'If now I have found favor in your eyes, give me a sign that it is really you talking to me.'"

PRAYER:

Father, in the name of Jesus Christ, I decree and declare that I have found favor in Your eyes, and You will give me a sign of Your favor at work in my life.

DAILY REFLECTION:

Take a moment to reflect on the Bible verse(s) for today and write your thoughts below:

BIBLE VERSE(S):

Matthew 5:6 AMP

"Blessed [joyful, nourished by God's goodness] are those who hunger and thirst for righteousness [those who actively seek right standing with God], for they will be [completely] satisfied."

PRAYER:

Father, in the name of Jesus Christ, I decree and declare that I am blessed, joyful, and nourished by Your goodness. I enjoy the favor and salvation of God, for I hunger and thirst for righteousness and I will be completely satisfied.

DAILY REFLECTION:

Take a moment to reflect on the Bible verse(s) for today and write your thoughts below:

February 13

BIBLE VERSE(S):

Psalm 119:132 ESV

"Turn to me and be gracious to me, as is your way with those who love your name."

PRAYER:

Father, in the name of Jesus Christ, I decree and declare that You shall turn to me and be gracious to me as is Your way with those who love Your name.

DAILY REFLECTION:

Take a moment to reflect on the Bible verse(s) for today and write your thoughts below:

BIBLE VERSE(S):

John 1:17 AMP

"For the Law was given through Moses, but grace [the unearned, undeserved favor of God] and truth came through Jesus Christ."

PRAYER:

Father, in the name of Jesus Christ, I thank You for granting me grace—Your unearned, undeserved favor—and truth through Jesus Christ, Your Son.

DAILY REFLECTION:

Take a moment to reflect on the Bible verse(s) for today and write your thoughts below:

February 15

BIBLE VERSE(S):

John 1:16 AMP

"For out of His fullness [the superabundance of His grace and truth] we have all received grace upon grace [spiritual blessing upon spiritual blessing, favor upon favor, and gift heaped upon gift]."

PRAYER:

Father, in the name of Jesus Christ, I decree and declare that out of Your superabundant grace and truth, I have received grace upon grace, spiritual blessing upon spiritual blessing, favor upon favor, and gift heaped upon gift. Lord God, I am very grateful.

DAILY REFLECTION:

Take a moment to reflect on the Bible verse(s) for today and write your thoughts below:

February 16

BIBLE VERSE(S):

2 Peter 3:18 AMP

"...but grow [spiritually mature] in the grace and knowledge of our Lord and Savior Jesus Christ. To Him be glory (honor, majesty, splendor), both now and to the day of eternity. Amen."

PRAYER:

Father, in the name of Jesus Christ, I decree and declare that I shall continue to grow in the grace and knowledge of our Lord and Savior, Jesus Christ. To Him be glory, honor, majesty, and splendor both now and to the day of eternity. Amen

DAILY REFLECTION:

Take a moment to reflect on the Bible verse(s) for today and write your thoughts below:

February 17

BIBLE VERSE(S):

2 Peter 1:2 NLT

"May God give you more and more grace and peace as you grow in your knowledge of God and Jesus our Lord."

PRAYER:

Father, in the name of Jesus Christ, I decree and declare that You shall give me more and more grace and peace as I grow in my knowledge of You, God, and Jesus Christ my Lord.

DAILY REFLECTION:

Take a moment to reflect on the Bible verse(s) for today and write your thoughts below:

BIBLE VERSE(S):

Proverbs 3:4-5 TLB

"If you want favor with both God and man, and a reputation for good judgment and common sense, then trust the Lord completely; don't ever trust yourself."

PRAYER:

Father, in the name of Jesus Christ, I want favor with both You and man, and a reputation for good judgment and common sense, so help me to trust You completely, Lord, and not ever trust myself.

DAILY REFLECTION:

Take a moment to reflect on the Bible verse(s) for today and write your thoughts below:

BIBLE VERSE(S):

Proverbs 8:35 NLT

"For whoever finds me [wisdom[2]] finds life and receives favor from the Lord."

PRAYER:

Father, in the name of Jesus Christ, I ask that You help me find wisdom that I may receive favor from You.

DAILY REFLECTION:

Take a moment to reflect on the Bible verse(s) for today and write your thoughts below:

2 My emphasis as this scripture refers to finding wisdom.

February 20

BIBLE VERSE(S):

Isaiah 61:2 NLT

"He has sent me to tell those who mourn that the time of the Lord's favor has come, and with it, the day of God's anger against their enemies."

PRAYER:

Father, in the name of Jesus Christ, I thank You that the time of Your favor has come in my life and with it, the day of Your anger against my enemies.

DAILY REFLECTION:

Take a moment to reflect on the Bible verse(s) for today and write your thoughts below:

February 21

BIBLE VERSE(S):

Acts 7:10 NLT

"And God gave him favor before Pharaoh, king of Egypt. God also gave Joseph unusual wisdom, so that Pharaoh appointed him governor over all of Egypt and put him in charge of the palace."

PRAYER:

Father, in the name of Jesus Christ, I ask that You give me favor and unusual wisdom, just as You gave Joseph.

DAILY REFLECTION:

Take a moment to reflect on the Bible verse(s) for today and write your thoughts below:

BIBLE VERSE(S):

Acts 7:46 NLT

"David found favor with God and asked for the privilege of building a permanent Temple for the God of Jacob."

PRAYER:

Father, in the name of Jesus Christ, just as David found favor with You, I ask that I find favor with You too.

DAILY REFLECTION:

Take a moment to reflect on the Bible verse(s) for today and write your thoughts below:

BIBLE VERSE(S):

Exodus 3:21 NLT

"And I will cause the Egyptians to look favorably on you. They will give you gifts when you go so you will not leave empty-handed."

PRAYER:

Father, in the name of Jesus Christ, I ask that you cause people to look favorably on me everywhere I go and cause me to never leave empty-handed.

DAILY REFLECTION:

Take a moment to reflect on the Bible verse(s) for today and write your thoughts below:

BIBLE VERSE(S):

Exodus 12:36 NLT

"The Lord caused the Egyptians to look favorably on the Israelites, and they gave the Israelites whatever they asked for. So they stripped the Egyptians of their wealth!"

PRAYER:

Father, in the name of Jesus Christ, I ask that You cause people to look favorably on me and give me whatever I ask for according to Your perfect will for my life and destiny.

DAILY REFLECTION:

Take a moment to reflect on the Bible verse(s) for today and write your thoughts below:

BIBLE VERSE(S):

Numbers 6:26 NLT

"May the Lord show you his favor and give you his peace."

PRAYER:

Father, in the name of Jesus Christ, I ask that You show me Your favor and give me Your peace.

DAILY REFLECTION:

Take a moment to reflect on the Bible verse(s) for today and write your thoughts below:

February 26

BIBLE VERSE(S):

1 Samuel 2:26 NLT

"Meanwhile, the boy Samuel grew taller and grew in favor with the Lord and with the people."

PRAYER:

Father, in the name of Jesus Christ, I decree and declare that I shall grow taller and grow in favor with You and with people just like Samuel.[3]

DAILY REFLECTION:

Take a moment to reflect on the Bible verse(s) for today and write your thoughts below:

3 If you have a child or children in your life, you can personalize this prayer for them.

February 27

BIBLE VERSE(S):

Psalm 9:4 NLT

"For you have judged in my favor; from your throne you have judged with fairness."

PRAYER:

Father, in the name of Jesus Christ, I thank You for judging in my favor; from Your throne, You have judged with fairness.

DAILY REFLECTION:

Take a moment to reflect on the Bible verse(s) for today and write your thoughts below:

BIBLE VERSE(S):

1 Corinthians 15:10 NLT

"But whatever I am now, it is all because God poured out his special favor on me—and not without results. For I have worked harder than any of the other apostles; yet it was not I but God who was working through me by his grace."

PRAYER:

Father, in the name of Jesus Christ, I thank You that whatever I am now is because You have poured out Your special favor on me. Thank You Lord. I am grateful for Your favor.

DAILY REFLECTION:

Take a moment to reflect on the Bible verse(s) for today and write your thoughts below:

BIBLE VERSE(S):

Romans 11:7 NLT

"So this is the situation: Most of the people of Israel have not found the favor of God they are looking for so earnestly. A few have—the ones God has chosen—but the hearts of the rest were hardened."

PRAYER:

Father, in the name of Jesus Christ, I ask that You choose me that I may always find Your favor.

DAILY REFLECTION:

Take a moment to reflect on the Bible verse(s) for today and write your thoughts below:

Heavenly Father, do marvelous things for us in the month of March and beyond in Jesus name.

CHAPTER 3

Marvelous **March**

He does great things too marvelous to understand. He performs countless miracles.
Job 5:9 NLT

Welcome to Marvelous March!

God is so wonderful, and His deeds are marvelous. This month, as you explore and make declarations about the marvelous deeds of God as recorded in the Bible, I pray that you will experience more of His marvelous deeds in and through your life, in the name of Jesus Christ.

March 1

BIBLE VERSE(S):

1 Chronicles 16:24 NIV

"Declare his glory among the nations, his marvelous deeds among all peoples."

PRAYER:

Father, in the name of Jesus Christ, I declare Your glory among the nations, Your marvelous deeds among all peoples. I thank You that in this month of March, I shall experience more and more of Your marvelous deeds in my life. Lord, Your marvelous deeds are good, pleasing, splendid, wonderful, and glorious. I decree and declare that the marvelous deeds of God shall never depart from my life and all that concerns me, in the mighty name of Jesus Christ.

DAILY REFLECTION:

Take a moment to reflect on the Bible verse(s) for today and write your thoughts below:

BIBLE VERSE(S):

Job 37:5 NIV

"God's voice thunders in marvelous ways; he does great things beyond our understanding."

PRAYER:

Father, in the name of Jesus Christ, let Your voice thunder in marvelous ways. I ask that You do great things in and around my life beyond my understanding.

DAILY REFLECTION:

Take a moment to reflect on the Bible verse(s) for today and write your thoughts below:

BIBLE VERSE(S):

Psalm 71:17 NIV

"Since my youth, God, you have taught me, and to this day I declare your marvelous deeds."

PRAYER:

Father, in the name of Jesus Christ, I ask that You continue to teach me, as I continue to declare Your marvelous deeds.

DAILY REFLECTION:

Take a moment to reflect on the Bible verse(s) for today and write your thoughts below:

March 4

BIBLE VERSE(S):

Psalm 72:18 NIV

"Praise be to the Lord God, the God of Israel, who alone does marvelous deeds."

PRAYER:

Father, in the name of Jesus Christ, I praise You, Lord God of Israel, who alone does marvelous deeds.

DAILY REFLECTION:

Take a moment to reflect on the Bible verse(s) for today and write your thoughts below:

March 5

BIBLE VERSE(S):

Psalm 86:10 NIV

"For you are great and do marvelous deeds; you alone are God."

PRAYER:

Father, in the name of Jesus Christ, I ask that You do great and marvelous deeds in my life and destiny, for You alone are God.

DAILY REFLECTION:

Take a moment to reflect on the Bible verse(s) for today and write your thoughts below:

March 6

BIBLE VERSE(S):

Psalm 96:3 NIV

"Declare his glory among the nations, his marvelous deeds among all peoples."

PRAYER:

Father, in the name of Jesus Christ, I declare Your glory among the nations and Your marvelous deeds among all peoples.

DAILY REFLECTION:

Take a moment to reflect on the Bible verse(s) for today and write your thoughts below:

March 7

BIBLE VERSE(S):

Psalm 98:1 NIV

"Sing to the Lord a new song, for he has done marvelous things; his right hand and his holy arm have worked salvation for him."

PRAYER:

Father, in the name of Jesus Christ, I sing a new song[4] to You, Lord, for You have done marvelous things.

DAILY REFLECTION:

Take a moment to reflect on the Bible verse(s) for today and write your thoughts below:

4 Make sure to sing a song of praise to the Lord for the marvelous things He has done.

March 8

BIBLE VERSE(S):

Psalm 118:23 NIV

"The Lord has done this, and it is marvelous in our eyes."

PRAYER:

Father, in the name of Jesus Christ, I thank You for all You have done for me. It is marvelous in my eyes.

DAILY REFLECTION:

Take a moment to reflect on the Bible verse(s) for today and write your thoughts below:

BIBLE VERSE(S):

Mark 12:11 NIV

"'The Lord has done this, and it is marvelous in our eyes'?"

PRAYER:

Father, in the name of Jesus Christ, I acknowledge that You are the doer of the marvelous things I see in and around my life. I am so grateful. Thank You Lord.

DAILY REFLECTION:

Take a moment to reflect on the Bible verse(s) for today and write your thoughts below:

BIBLE VERSE(S):

Matthew 21:42 NIV

"Jesus said to them, 'Have you never read in the Scriptures: "The stone the builders rejected has become the cornerstone; the Lord has done this, and it is marvelous in our eyes"?'"

PRAYER:

Father, in the name of Jesus Christ, I thank You for making me become the cornerstone. It is Your doing Lord, and it is marvelous in my eyes.

DAILY REFLECTION:

Take a moment to reflect on the Bible verse(s) for today and write your thoughts below:

March 11

BIBLE VERSE(S):

Revelation 15:3 NIV

"And sang the song of God's servant Moses and of the Lamb: 'Great and marvelous are your deeds, Lord God Almighty. Just and true are your ways, King of the nations.'"

PRAYER:

Father, in the name of Jesus Christ, I praise You, for Your deeds are great and marvelous and Your ways are just and true.

DAILY REFLECTION:

Take a moment to reflect on the Bible verse(s) for today and write your thoughts below:

March 12

BIBLE VERSE(S):

Psalm 78:1-4 MSG

"Listen, dear friends, to God's truth, bend your ears to what I tell you. I'm chewing on the morsel of a proverb; I'll let you in on the sweet old truths, Stories we heard from our fathers, counsel we learned at our mother's knee. We're not keeping this to ourselves, we're passing it along to the next generation— God's fame and fortune, the marvelous things he has done."

PRAYER:

Father, in the name of Jesus Christ, I ask for the grace to pass along to the next generation Your fame and fortune and the marvelous things You have done.

DAILY REFLECTION:

Take a moment to reflect on the Bible verse(s) for today and write your thoughts below:

March 13

BIBLE VERSE(S):

Psalm 107:4-9 MSG

"Some of you wandered for years in the desert, looking but not finding a good place to live, Half-starved and parched with thirst, staggering and stumbling, on the brink of exhaustion. Then, in your desperate condition, you called out to God. He got you out in the nick of time; He put your feet on a wonderful road that took you straight to a good place to live. So thank God for his marvelous love, for his miracle mercy to the children he loves. He poured great drafts of water down parched throats; the starved and hungry got plenty to eat."

PRAYER:

Father, in the name of Jesus Christ, I thank You for Your marvelous love and Your miracle of mercy at work in my life and destiny.

DAILY REFLECTION:

Take a moment to reflect on the Bible verse(s) for today and write your thoughts below:

March 14

BIBLE VERSE(S):

Psalm 107:10-16 MSG

"Some of you were locked in a dark cell, cruelly confined behind bars, Punished for defying God's Word, for turning your back on the High God's counsel— A hard sentence, and your hearts so heavy, and not a soul in sight to help. Then you called out to God in your desperate condition; he got you out in the nick of time. He led you out of your dark, dark cell, broke open the jail and led you out. So thank God for his marvelous love, for his miracle mercy to the children he loves; He shattered the heavy jailhouse doors, he snapped the prison bars like matchsticks!"

PRAYER:

Father, in the name of Jesus Christ, I thank You for Your marvelous love and miracle of mercy. Thank You, God, for getting me out in the nick of time when I called out to You in my desperate condition.

DAILY REFLECTION:

Take a moment to reflect on the Bible verse(s) for today and write your thoughts below:

BIBLE VERSE(S):

Psalm 107:17-22 MSG

"Some of you were sick because you'd lived a bad life, your bodies feeling the effects of your sin; You couldn't stand the sight of food, so miserable you thought you'd be better off dead. Then you called out to God in your desperate condition; he got you out in the nick of time. He spoke the word that healed you, that pulled you back from the brink of death. So thank God for his marvelous love, for his miracle mercy to the children he loves; Offer thanksgiving sacrifices, tell the world what he's done—sing it out!"

PRAYER:

Father, in the name of Jesus Christ, I thank You for Your marvelous love and miracle of mercy. I am so grateful! I will tell the world what You have done!

DAILY REFLECTION:

Take a moment to reflect on the Bible verse(s) for today and write your thoughts below:

March 16

BIBLE VERSE(S):

Psalm 145:6 MSG

"Your marvelous doings are headline news; I could write a book full of the details of your greatness."

PRAYER:

Father, in the name of Jesus Christ, I thank You for your marvelous doings. Words are not even sufficient to describe the details of Your greatness. I just want to say Thank You, Lord, for You are great.

DAILY REFLECTION:

Take a moment to reflect on the Bible verse(s) for today and write your thoughts below:

BIBLE VERSE(S):

Jeremiah 33:2-3 MSG

"This is God's Message, the God who made earth, made it livable and lasting, known everywhere as God: 'Call to me and I will answer you. I'll tell you marvelous and wondrous things that you could never figure out on your own.'"

PRAYER:

Father, in the name of Jesus Christ, I thank You that You answer me when I call to You. Father, I ask that You tell me marvelous and wondrous things that I could never figure out on my own.

DAILY REFLECTION:

Take a moment to reflect on the Bible verse(s) for today and write your thoughts below:

March 18

BIBLE VERSE(S):

Psalm 139:13-16 MSG

"Oh yes, you shaped me first inside, then out; you formed me in my mother's womb. I thank you, High God—you're breathtaking! Body and soul, I am marvelously made! I worship in adoration—what a creation! You know me inside and out, you know every bone in my body; You know exactly how I was made, bit by bit, how I was sculpted from nothing into something. Like an open book, you watched me grow from conception to birth; all the stages of my life were spread out before you, The days of my life all prepared before I'd even lived one day."

PRAYER:

Father, in the name of Jesus Christ, I thank You for making me marvelously. You are an amazing God.

DAILY REFLECTION:

Take a moment to reflect on the Bible verse(s) for today and write your thoughts below:

____

____

____

____

____

BIBLE VERSE(S):

Acts 20:32 MSG

"Now I'm turning you over to God, our marvelous God whose gracious Word can make you into what he wants you to be and give you everything you could possibly need in this community of holy friends."

PRAYER:

Our Marvelous God, I ask in the name of Jesus Christ that by Your Word You make me into what You want me to be and give me everything I could possibly need in my life and destiny.

DAILY REFLECTION:

Take a moment to reflect on the Bible verse(s) for today and write your thoughts below:

BIBLE VERSE(S):

1 Corinthians 7:20-22 MSG

"Stay where you were when God called your name. Were you a slave? Slavery is no roadblock to obeying and believing. I don't mean you're stuck and can't leave. If you have a chance at freedom, go ahead and take it. I'm simply trying to point out that under your new Master you're going to experience a marvelous freedom you would never have dreamed of. On the other hand, if you were free when Christ called you, you'll experience a delightful "enslavement to God" you would never have dreamed of."

PRAYER:

Father, in the name of Jesus Christ, I thank You for the marvelous freedom I experience under You as my Master.

DAILY REFLECTION:

Take a moment to reflect on the Bible verse(s) for today and write your thoughts below:

March 21

BIBLE VERSE(S):

1 John 3:1 MSG

"What marvelous love the Father has extended to us! Just look at it—we're called children of God! That's who we really are. But that's also why the world doesn't recognize us or take us seriously, because it has no idea who he is or what he's up to."

PRAYER:

Father, in the name of Jesus Christ, I thank You for extending Your marvelous love to me and for calling me Your child.

DAILY REFLECTION:

Take a moment to reflect on the Bible verse(s) for today and write your thoughts below:

March 22

BIBLE VERSE(S):

Job 9:10 NLT

"He does great things too marvelous to understand. He performs countless miracles."

PRAYER:

Father, in the name of Jesus Christ, I decree and declare that You will do things in my life too marvelous for people to understand. Thank You, Jesus, for performing countless miracles in my life.

DAILY REFLECTION:

Take a moment to reflect on the Bible verse(s) for today and write your thoughts below:

____

____

____

____

____

____

____

____

____

____

March 23

BIBLE VERSE(S):

Psalm 145:12 NIV

"...so that all people may know of your mighty acts and the glorious splendor of your kingdom."

PRAYER:

Father, in the name of Jesus Christ, I decree and declare that I shall know of Your mighty acts and the glorious splendor of Your kingdom.

DAILY REFLECTION:

Take a moment to reflect on the Bible verse(s) for today and write your thoughts below:

BIBLE VERSE(S):

Job 5:8-9 ESV

"As for me, I would seek God, and to God would I commit my cause, who does great things and unsearchable, marvelous things without number:"

PRAYER:

Father, in the name of Jesus Christ, I seek You today and commit my cause to You, for You do great, unsearchable, and marvelous things without number.

DAILY REFLECTION:

Take a moment to reflect on the Bible verse(s) for today and write your thoughts below:

March 25

BIBLE VERSE(S):

1 Chronicles 16:24-25 ESV

"Declare his glory among the nations, his marvelous works among all the peoples! For great is the Lord, and greatly to be praised, and he is to be feared above all gods."

PRAYER:

Father, in the name of Jesus Christ, I declare Your glory among the nations, Your marvelous works among all the peoples. For You are great and greatly to be praised.

DAILY REFLECTION:

Take a moment to reflect on the Bible verse(s) for today and write your thoughts below:

March 26

BIBLE VERSE(S):

Micah 7:15 ESV

"As in the days when you came out of the land of Egypt, I will show them marvelous things."

PRAYER:

Father, in the name of Jesus Christ, I ask that You show me marvelous things all the days of my life.

DAILY REFLECTION:

Take a moment to reflect on the Bible verse(s) for today and write your thoughts below:

BIBLE VERSE(S):

1 Peter 2:9 ESV

"But you are a chosen race, a royal priesthood, a holy nation, a people for his own possession, that you may proclaim the excellencies of him who called you out of darkness into his marvelous light."

PRAYER:

Father, in the name of Jesus Christ, I thank You for calling me out of darkness into Your marvelous light. I decree and declare that Your word in 1 Peter 2:9 finds full expression in my life now and always.

DAILY REFLECTION:

Take a moment to reflect on the Bible verse(s) for today and write your thoughts below:

March 28

BIBLE VERSE(S):

Psalm 19:1 TLB

"The heavens are telling the glory of God; they are a marvelous display of his craftsmanship."

PRAYER:

Father, in the name of Jesus Christ, just as the heavens tell of Your glory; a marvelous display of Your craftsmanship, let my life tell of Your glory and be a marvelous display of Your craftmanship.

DAILY REFLECTION:

Take a moment to reflect on the Bible verse(s) for today and write your thoughts below:

BIBLE VERSE(S):

Psalm 139:14 TLB

"Thank you for making me so wonderfully complex! It is amazing to think about. Your workmanship is marvelous—and how well I know it."

PRAYER:

Father, in the name of Jesus Christ, I thank You for making me so wonderfully complex. Your workmanship is indeed marvelous.

DAILY REFLECTION:

Take a moment to reflect on the Bible verse(s) for today and write your thoughts below:

March 30

BIBLE VERSE(S):

Ephesians 3:17 TLB

"And I pray that Christ will be more and more at home in your hearts, living within you as you trust in him. May your roots go down deep into the soil of God's marvelous love;"

PRAYER:

Father, in the name of Jesus Christ, let Christ be more and more at home in my heart, living within me as I trust in Him. May my roots go down deep into the soil of God's marvelous love.

DAILY REFLECTION:

Take a moment to reflect on the Bible verse(s) for today and write your thoughts below:

March 31

BIBLE VERSE(S):

2 Chronicles 26:15 EXB

"In Jerusalem Uzziah made ·cleverly [expertly; carefully] designed ·devices [machines]. These ·devices [machines] on the towers and corners of the city walls were used to shoot arrows and large rocks. So Uzziah became famous in faraway places, because he ·had much help until he became [was marvelously/tremendously helped to become] powerful."

2 Chronicles 26:15 NLT

"And he built structures on the walls of Jerusalem, designed by experts to protect those who shot arrows and hurled large stones from the towers and the corners of the wall. His fame spread far and wide, for the Lord gave him marvelous help, and he became very powerful."

PRAYER:

Father, in the name of Jesus Christ, I ask that You marvelously help me, just as You helped Uzziah, until I become very powerful.

DAILY REFLECTION:

Take a moment to reflect on the Bible verse(s) for today and write your thoughts below:

Father in the name of Jesus, let us have encounters with You, and through Your word that will leave us astonished in the month of April and beyond in Jesus name.

CHAPTER 4

Astonishing April

Then He went down to Capernaum, a city of Galilee, and was teaching them on the Sabbaths. And they were astonished at His teaching, for His word was with authority.
Luke 4:31-32 NKJV

Welcome to Astonishing April!

God is absolutely incredible. In Astonishing April, you will delve into a deeper dimension of God's ability to bless us in astonishing ways as recorded in Scriptures.

Get ready to receive pleasant surprises, astonishing blessings, and amazing breakthroughs as you pray and declare the astonishing promises of God over your life.

BIBLE VERSE(S):

2 Corinthians 9:8-11 MSG

"God can pour on the blessings in astonishing ways so that you're ready for anything and everything, more than just ready to do what needs to be done. As one psalmist puts it, He throws caution to the winds, giving to the needy in reckless abandon. His right-living, right-giving ways never run out, never wear out. This most generous God who gives seed to the farmer that becomes bread for your meals is more than extravagant with you. He gives you something you can then give away, which grows into full-formed lives, robust in God, wealthy in every way, so that you can be generous in every way, producing with us great praise to God."

PRAYER:

Father, in the name of Jesus Christ, I ask that You pour out Your blessings on me in astonishing ways so that I am ready for anything and everything, more than just ready to do what needs to be done.

DAILY REFLECTION:

Take a moment to reflect on the Bible verse(s) for today and write your thoughts below:

____

____

____

BIBLE VERSE(S):

Daniel 6:25-27 MSG

"King Darius published this proclamation to every race, color, and creed on earth: Peace to you! Abundant peace! I decree that Daniel's God shall be worshiped and feared in all parts of my kingdom. He is the living God, world without end. His kingdom never falls. His rule continues eternally. He is a savior and rescuer. He performs astonishing miracles in heaven and on earth. He saved Daniel from the power of the lions."

PRAYER:

Father, in the name of Jesus Christ, I ask that You perform astonishing miracles in my life. Save me as You saved Daniel from the power of the lions.

DAILY REFLECTION:

Take a moment to reflect on the Bible verse(s) for today and write your thoughts below:

BIBLE VERSE(S):

Isaiah 29:14 AMP

"Therefore, listen carefully, I will again do marvelous and amazing things with this people, wonderful and astonishing things; And the wisdom of their wise men will perish, And the understanding of their discerning men will be hidden."

PRAYER:

Father, in the name of Jesus Christ, I decree and declare that You will do marvelous, amazing, wonderful and astonishing things in my life.

DAILY REFLECTION:

Take a moment to reflect on the Bible verse(s) for today and write your thoughts below:

BIBLE VERSE(S):

John 9:30 AMP

"The man replied, 'Well, this is astonishing! You do not know where He comes from, and yet He opened my eyes!'"

PRAYER:

Father, in the name of Jesus Christ, I ask that Your works be astonishing in my life, to my surprise and the amazement of other people.

DAILY REFLECTION:

Take a moment to reflect on the Bible verse(s) for today and write your thoughts below:

BIBLE VERSE(S):

2 Corinthians 8:9 AMP

"For you are recognizing [more clearly] the grace of our Lord Jesus Christ [His astonishing kindness, His generosity, His gracious favor], that though He was rich, yet for your sake He became poor, so that by His poverty you might become rich (abundantly blessed)."

PRAYER:

Father, in the name of Jesus Christ, let me recognize, more clearly, the grace of our Lord Jesus Christ—His astonishing kindness, His generosity, His gracious favor—that though He was rich, yet for our sake He became poor, so that by His poverty I might become abundantly blessed.

DAILY REFLECTION:

Take a moment to reflect on the Bible verse(s) for today and write your thoughts below:

BIBLE VERSE(S):

Job 26:11 ESV

"The pillars of heaven tremble and are astounded at his rebuke."

PRAYER:

Father, in the name of Jesus Christ, with the awareness that the pillars of the heavens tremble and are astounded at Your rebuke, I decree and declare that I will remain mindful of Your astonishing power.

DAILY REFLECTION:

Take a moment to reflect on the Bible verse(s) for today and write your thoughts below:

BIBLE VERSE(S):

Habakkuk 1:5 AMP

"[The Lord replied,] 'Look among the nations! See! Be astonished! Wonder! For I am doing something in your days—You would not believe it if you were told.'"

PRAYER:

Father, in the name of Jesus Christ, I thank You for the astonishing things You are doing amongst the nations in my days.

DAILY REFLECTION:

Take a moment to reflect on the Bible verse(s) for today and write your thoughts below:

BIBLE VERSE(S):

Matthew 22:33 NIV

"When the crowds heard this, they were astonished at his teaching."

PRAYER:

Father, in the name of Jesus Christ, let me be always astonished at Your teaching. Let my astonishment never cease or wear out.

DAILY REFLECTION:

Take a moment to reflect on the Bible verse(s) for today and write your thoughts below:

BIBLE VERSE(S):

Luke 11:38 AMP

"The Pharisee noticed this and was surprised that Jesus did not first ceremonially wash before the meal."

PRAYER:

Father, in the name of Jesus Christ, I ask that You lead me and guide my actions, that they would not be ceremonial. Let all who see my actions be astonished because my actions will be guided by You.

DAILY REFLECTION:

Take a moment to reflect on the Bible verse(s) for today and write your thoughts below:

BIBLE VERSE(S):

Luke 20:26 NIV

"They were unable to trap him in what he had said there in public. And astonished by his answer, they became silent."

PRAYER:

Father, in the name of Jesus Christ, I ask that You guard my mouth and my words. Let my speech be always full of Your grace and astonishment.

DAILY REFLECTION:

Take a moment to reflect on the Bible verse(s) for today and write your thoughts below:

BIBLE VERSE(S):

John 7:21 AMP

"Jesus replied, 'I did one [The healing of the paralytic at Bethesda occurred during Jesus' last visit to Jerusalem.] work, and you are all astounded.'"

PRAYER:

Father, in the name of Jesus Christ, I ask that You do one work in my life and let all be astonished.

DAILY REFLECTION:

Take a moment to reflect on the Bible verse(s) for today and write your thoughts below:

BIBLE VERSE(S):

Acts 8:13 NIV

"Simon himself believed and was baptized. And he followed Philip everywhere, astonished by the great signs and miracles he saw."

PRAYER:

Father, in the name of Jesus Christ, I decree and declare that I will see firsthand signs and great miracles in my life that will leave me astonished.

DAILY REFLECTION:

Take a moment to reflect on the Bible verse(s) for today and write your thoughts below:

April 13

BIBLE VERSE(S):

Acts 10:45 NIV

"The circumcised believers who had come with Peter were astonished that the gift of the Holy Spirit had been poured out even on Gentiles."

PRAYER:

Father, in the name of Jesus Christ, I decree and declare that the outpouring of the gift of the Holy Spirit in my life will be so astonishing.

DAILY REFLECTION:

Take a moment to reflect on the Bible verse(s) for today and write your thoughts below:

BIBLE VERSE(S):

Acts 13:11-12 ESV

"'And now, behold, the hand of the Lord is upon you, and you will be blind and unable to see the sun for a time.' Immediately mist and darkness fell upon him, and he went about seeking people to lead him by the hand. Then the proconsul believed, when he saw what had occurred, for he was astonished at the teaching of the Lord."

PRAYER:

Father, in the name of Jesus Christ, I decree and declare that more people will come to believe and be astonished by the teaching about the Lord Jesus in the nations of the earth.

DAILY REFLECTION:

Take a moment to reflect on the Bible verse(s) for today and write your thoughts below:

BIBLE VERSE(S):

Mark 5:42 NIV

"Immediately the girl stood up and began to walk around (she was twelve years old). At this they were completely astonished."

PRAYER:

Father, in the name of Jesus Christ, I thank You for the miraculous healing of the twelve-year-old girl. I decree and declare that I will experience your numerous miracles which will leave me astonished in the mighty name of Jesus Christ.

DAILY REFLECTION:

Take a moment to reflect on the Bible verse(s) for today and write your thoughts below:

BIBLE VERSE(S):

Luke 1:62-64 NIV

"Then they made signs to his father, to find out what he would like to name the child. He asked for a writing tablet, and to everyone's astonishment he wrote, 'His name is John.' Immediately his mouth was opened and his tongue set free, and he began to speak, praising God."

PRAYER:

Father, in the name of Jesus Christ, I ask that You perform great works in and through my life to everyone's astonishment.

DAILY REFLECTION:

Take a moment to reflect on the Bible verse(s) for today and write your thoughts below:

BIBLE VERSE(S):

Luke 2:47-49 NIV

"Everyone who heard him was amazed at his understanding and his answers. When his parents saw him, they were astonished. His mother said to him, 'Son, why have you treated us like this? Your father and I have been anxiously searching for you.' 'Why were you searching for me?' he asked. 'Didn't you know I had to be in my Father's house?'"

PRAYER:

Father, in the name of Jesus Christ, let everyone who hears me be amazed and let everyone who sees me be astonished due to my understanding, which comes from Your Holy Spirit.

DAILY REFLECTION:

Take a moment to reflect on the Bible verse(s) for today and write your thoughts below:

BIBLE VERSE(S):

Luke 5:8-10 NIV

"When Simon Peter saw this, he fell at Jesus' knees and said, 'Go away from me, Lord; I am a sinful man!' For he and all his companions were astonished at the catch of fish they had taken, and so were James and John, the sons of Zebedee, Simon's partners. Then Jesus said to Simon, 'Don't be afraid; from now on you will fish for people.'"

PRAYER:

Father, in the name of Jesus Christ, I ask that You perform great wonders in my life that will make all who see them astonished.

DAILY REFLECTION:

Take a moment to reflect on the Bible verse(s) for today and write your thoughts below:

BIBLE VERSE(S):

Luke 8:55-56 NIV

"Her spirit returned, and at once she stood up. Then Jesus told them to give her something to eat. Her parents were astonished, but he ordered them not to tell anyone what had happened."

PRAYER:

Father, in the name of Jesus Christ, I ask that You do mighty miracles in my life that will keep me astonished.

DAILY REFLECTION:

Take a moment to reflect on the Bible verse(s) for today and write your thoughts below:

BIBLE VERSE(S):

Acts 4:13 NIV

"When they saw the courage of Peter and John and realized that they were unschooled, ordinary men, they were astonished and they took note that these men had been with Jesus."

PRAYER:

Father, in the name of Jesus Christ, I ask that You bless me with courage, that all will be astonished and take note that I have been with Jesus Christ.

DAILY REFLECTION:

Take a moment to reflect on the Bible verse(s) for today and write your thoughts below:

BIBLE VERSE(S):

Acts 8:13 NIV

"Simon himself believed and was baptized. And he followed Philip everywhere, astonished by the great signs and miracles he saw."

PRAYER:

Father, in the name of Jesus Christ, let me see great signs and miracles everywhere that will leave me astonished.

DAILY REFLECTION:

Take a moment to reflect on the Bible verse(s) for today and write your thoughts below:

BIBLE VERSE(S):

Acts 10:45 NIV

"The circumcised believers who had come with Peter were astonished that the gift of the Holy Spirit had been poured out even on Gentiles."

PRAYER:

Father, in the name of Jesus Christ, I ask that all who encounter me will be astonished by the outpouring of the gift of the Holy Spirit on me.

DAILY REFLECTION:

Take a moment to reflect on the Bible verse(s) for today and write your thoughts below:

BIBLE VERSE(S):

John 5:20 NLT

"For the Father loves the Son and shows him everything he is doing. In fact, the Father will show him how to do even greater works than healing this man. Then you will truly be astonished."

PRAYER:

Father, in the name of Jesus Christ, just as You love Jesus Christ and show Him everything that You are doing, I ask that You show me how to do even greater works, and that everyone will be astonished.

DAILY REFLECTION:

Take a moment to reflect on the Bible verse(s) for today and write your thoughts below:

BIBLE VERSE(S):

Acts 13:12 NLT

"When the governor saw what had happened, he became a believer, for he was astonished at the teaching about the Lord."

PRAYER:

Father, in the name of Jesus Christ, let me be constantly astonished by the teachings of the Lord.

DAILY REFLECTION:

Take a moment to reflect on the Bible verse(s) for today and write your thoughts below:

BIBLE VERSE(S):

Psalm 46:8-10 MSG

"Attention, all! See the marvels of God! He plants flowers and trees all over the earth, Bans war from pole to pole, breaks all the weapons across his knee. 'Step out of the traffic! Take a long, loving look at me, your High God, above politics, above everything.'"

PRAYER:

Father, in the name of Jesus Christ, I decree and declare that I shall continue to see the marvels of God in my life. I will take a long, loving look at My High God above everything.

DAILY REFLECTION:

Take a moment to reflect on the Bible verse(s) for today and write your thoughts below:

BIBLE VERSE(S):

Daniel 3:24 ESV

"Then King Nebuchadnezzar was astonished and rose up in haste. He declared to his counselors, 'Did we not cast three men bound into the fire?' They answered and said to the king, 'True, O king.' He answered and said, 'But I see four men unbound, walking in the midst of the fire, and they are not hurt; and the appearance of the fourth is like a son of the gods.'"

PRAYER:

Father, in the name of Jesus Christ, just like King Nebuchadnezzar was astonished, let me and others be astonished by Your great wonders in my life.

DAILY REFLECTION:

Take a moment to reflect on the Bible verse(s) for today and write your thoughts below:

BIBLE VERSE(S):

Matthew 7:28 AMP

"When Jesus had finished [speaking] these words [on the mountain], the crowds were astonished and overwhelmed at His teaching;"

PRAYER:

Father, in the name of Jesus Christ, I decree and declare that I will be constantly astonished by the teaching of Jesus Christ through His Word.

DAILY REFLECTION:

Take a moment to reflect on the Bible verse(s) for today and write your thoughts below:

BIBLE VERSE(S):

Mark 1:22 ESV

"And they were astonished at his teaching, for he taught them as one who had authority, and not as the scribes."

PRAYER:

Father, in the name of Jesus Christ, I ask that You give me divine encounters through Your Word. Let me be astonished at the teaching of Jesus as recorded in the Bible.

DAILY REFLECTION:

Take a moment to reflect on the Bible verse(s) for today and write your thoughts below:

BIBLE VERSE(S):

Mark 7:37 ESV

"And they were astonished beyond measure, saying, 'He has done all things well. He even makes the deaf hear and the mute speak.'"

PRAYER:

Father, in the name of Jesus Christ, let my life reflect the miraculous power of Jesus Christ, which will leave me astonished beyond measure.

DAILY REFLECTION:

Take a moment to reflect on the Bible verse(s) for today and write your thoughts below:

BIBLE VERSE(S):

Mark 2:11-13 AMP

"'I say to you, get up, pick up your mat and go home.' And he got up and immediately picked up the mat and went out before them all, so that they all were astonished and they glorified and praised God, saying, 'We have never seen anything like this!' Jesus went out again along the [Galilean] seashore; and all the people were coming to Him, and He was teaching them."

PRAYER:

Father, in the name of Jesus Christ, let me experience a never been seen before wonder in my life that will leave me astonished and glorify God saying – I have never seen anything like this!

DAILY REFLECTION:

Take a moment to reflect on the Bible verse(s) for today and write your thoughts below:

Father, in the name of Jesus, let our testimonies be magnificent in the month of May and beyond.

CHAPTER 5

Magnificent **May**

Sing to the Lord, for He has done magnificent things, let this be known throughout the earth!
Isaiah 12:5 NET

Welcome to Magnificent May!

I love the Scripture for the first day of May because it speaks volumes about the creative power of God at work in our lives, which enables us to conceive magnificent things.

Magnificent things can be described as very good, excellent, impressive, splendid, and admirable. I decree and declare that in the month of May, your blessings and testimonies shall be described as magnificent in the mighty name of Jesus Christ.

May 1

BIBLE VERSE(S):

Isaiah 32:8 AMP

"But the noble man conceives noble and magnificent things; And he stands by what is noble and magnificent."

PRAYER:

Father, in the name of Jesus Christ, I ask that You help me to conceive noble and magnificent things and stand by what is noble and magnificent.

DAILY REFLECTION:

Take a moment to reflect on the Bible verse(s) for today and write your thoughts below:

BIBLE VERSE(S):

Isaiah 28:5 AMP

"In that day the Lord of hosts will become a magnificent crown And a glorious diadem to the [converted] remnant of His people."

PRAYER:

Father, in the name of Jesus Christ, I thank You for becoming a magnificent crown and a glorious diadem to me and my family.

DAILY REFLECTION:

Take a moment to reflect on the Bible verse(s) for today and write your thoughts below:

BIBLE VERSE(S):

Isaiah 33:21 AMP

"But there the mighty and magnificent Lord will be for us A place of broad rivers and streams, where no oar-driven boat will go, And on which no mighty and stately ship will pass."

PRAYER:

Father, in the name of Jesus Christ, let me experience You as the mighty and magnificent Lord as You are for me a place of broad rivers and streams, where no oar-driven boat will go, and on which no mighty and stately ship will pass.

DAILY REFLECTION:

Take a moment to reflect on the Bible verse(s) for today and write your thoughts below:

BIBLE VERSE(S):

Isaiah 61:3 AMP

"To grant to those who mourn in Zion the following: To give them a turban instead of dust [on their heads, a sign of mourning], The oil of joy instead of mourning, The garment [expressive] of praise instead of a disheartened spirit. So they will be called the trees of righteousness [strong and magnificent, distinguished for integrity, justice, and right standing with God], The planting of the Lord, that He may be glorified."

PRAYER:

Father, in the name of Jesus Christ, I declare that I am called the tree of righteousness—strong and magnificent, distinguished for integrity, justice, and right standing with God—the planting of the Lord, that He may be glorified.

DAILY REFLECTION:

Take a moment to reflect on the Bible verse(s) for today and write your thoughts below:

May 5

BIBLE VERSE(S):

2 Peter 1:4 AMP

"For by these He has bestowed on us His precious and magnificent promises [of inexpressible value], so that by them you may escape from the immoral freedom that is in the world because of disreputable desire, and become sharers of the divine nature."

PRAYER:

Father, in the name of Jesus Christ, I thank You for Your precious and magnificent promises of inexpressible value, by which I escape from the immoral freedom in the world and become sharers of the divine nature.

DAILY REFLECTION:

Take a moment to reflect on the Bible verse(s) for today and write your thoughts below:

BIBLE VERSE(S):

Numbers 23:21-22 AMP

"God has not observed wickedness in Jacob [for he is forgiven], Nor has He seen trouble in Israel. The Lord their God is with Israel, And the shout of their King is among the people. God brought them out of Egypt; They have the strength of a wild ox."

PRAYER:

Father, in the name of Jesus Christ, I decree and declare that You will not observe wickedness in me for I am forgiven, nor will you see trouble in me. You are my Lord and God who delivers and strengthens me.

DAILY REFLECTION:

Take a moment to reflect on the Bible verse(s) for today and write your thoughts below:

BIBLE VERSE(S):

Psalm 111:2 AMP

"Great are the works of the Lord, Studied by all those who delight in them."

PRAYER:

Father, in the name of Jesus Christ, I thank You for Your great works, for I delight in them.

DAILY REFLECTION:

Take a moment to reflect on the Bible verse(s) for today and write your thoughts below:

BIBLE VERSE(S):

2 Peter 1:17 NIV

"He received honor and glory from God the Father when the voice came to him from the Majestic Glory, saying, 'This is my Son, whom I love; with him I am well pleased.'"

PRAYER:

Father, in the name of Jesus Christ, I ask that You fill me up with Your majestic glory. Let me be always pleasing to You.

DAILY REFLECTION:

Take a moment to reflect on the Bible verse(s) for today and write your thoughts below:

BIBLE VERSE(S):

Numbers 14:19 TLB

"Oh, I plead with you, pardon the sins of this people because of your magnificent, steadfast love, just as you have forgiven them all the time from when we left Egypt until now."

PRAYER:

Father, I ask that You pardon my sins because of Your magnificent, steadfast love in the name of Jesus Christ.

DAILY REFLECTION:

Take a moment to reflect on the Bible verse(s) for today and write your thoughts below:

BIBLE VERSE(S):

Psalm 43:3-4 MSG

"Give me your lantern and compass, give me a map, So I can find my way to the sacred mountain, to the place of your presence, To enter the place of worship, meet my exuberant God, Sing my thanks with a harp, magnificent God, my God."

PRAYER:

Father, in the name of Jesus Christ, I declare Your magnificence and I thank You for being a magnificent God, my God.

DAILY REFLECTION:

Take a moment to reflect on the Bible verse(s) for today and write your thoughts below:

BIBLE VERSE(S):

Psalm 92:4-9 MSG

"You made me so happy, God. I saw your work and I shouted for joy. How magnificent your work, God! How profound your thoughts! Dullards never notice what you do; fools never do get it. When the wicked popped up like weeds and all the evil men and women took over, You mowed them down, finished them off once and for all. You, God, are High and Eternal. Look at your enemies, God! Look at your enemies—ruined! Scattered to the winds, all those hirelings of evil!"

PRAYER:

Father, in the name of Jesus Christ, I ask that You cause me to see your work and shout for joy, saying, "How magnificent your work, God!"

DAILY REFLECTION:

Take a moment to reflect on the Bible verse(s) for today and write your thoughts below:

May 12

BIBLE VERSE(S):

Psalm 113:4-9 MSG

"God is higher than anything and anyone, outshining everything you can see in the skies. Who can compare with God, our God, so majestically enthroned, Surveying his magnificent heavens and earth? He picks up the poor from out of the dirt, rescues the forgotten who've been thrown out with the trash, Seats them among the honored guests, a place of honor among the brightest and best. He gives childless couples a family, gives them joy as the parents of children. Hallelujah!"

PRAYER:

Father, in the name of Jesus Christ, I thank You for being so majestically enthroned, surveying Your magnificent heavens and earth. For no one can compare with God. You, God, are higher than anything and anyone, outshining everything I can see in the skies.

DAILY REFLECTION:

Take a moment to reflect on the Bible verse(s) for today and write your thoughts below:

May 13

BIBLE VERSE(S):

Psalm 145:3 MSG

"God is magnificent; he can never be praised enough. There are no boundaries to his greatness."

PRAYER:

Father, in the name of Jesus Christ, I declare that You are magnificent; You can never be praised enough. There are no boundaries to Your greatness.

DAILY REFLECTION:

Take a moment to reflect on the Bible verse(s) for today and write your thoughts below:

BIBLE VERSE(S):

Psalm 150:1-6 MSG

"Hallelujah! Praise God in his holy house of worship, praise him under the open skies; Praise him for his acts of power, praise him for his magnificent greatness; Praise with a blast on the trumpet, praise by strumming soft strings; Praise him with castanets and dance, praise him with banjo and flute; Praise him with cymbals and a big bass drum, praise him with fiddles and mandolin. Let every living, breathing creature praise God! Hallelujah!"

PRAYER:

Hallelujah! I praise You, God, for Your acts of power and magnificent greatness. I praise You as a living, breathing creature. Praise God. Hallelujah!

DAILY REFLECTION:

Take a moment to reflect on the Bible verse(s) for today and write your thoughts below:

BIBLE VERSE(S):

Isaiah 40:25-26 MSG

" 'So—who is like me? Who holds a candle to me?' says The Holy. 'Look at the night skies: Who do you think made all this? Who marches this army of stars out each night, counts them off, calls each by name —so magnificent! so powerful!— and never overlooks a single one?' "

PRAYER:

Father, in the name of Jesus Christ, I thank you for being so magnificent and so powerful. There is no one like you. You alone are God almighty.

DAILY REFLECTION:

Take a moment to reflect on the Bible verse(s) for today and write your thoughts below:

BIBLE VERSE(S):

Romans 8:1-2 MSG

"The Solution Is Life on God's Terms. With the arrival of Jesus, the Messiah, that fateful dilemma is resolved. Those who enter into Christ's being-here-for-us no longer have to live under a continuous, low-lying black cloud. A new power is in operation. The Spirit of life in Christ, like a strong wind, has magnificently cleared the air, freeing you from a fated lifetime of brutal tyranny at the hands of sin and death."

PRAYER:

Father, in the name of Jesus Christ, I decree and declare that the Spirit of life in Christ, like a strong wind, has magnificently cleared the air, freeing me from a fated lifetime of brutal tyranny at the hands of sin and death.

DAILY REFLECTION:

Take a moment to reflect on the Bible verse(s) for today and write your thoughts below:

____

____

____

____

____

____

BIBLE VERSE(S):

Ephesians 3:14-19 MSG

"My response is to get down on my knees before the Father, this magnificent Father who parcels out all heaven and earth. I ask him to strengthen you by his Spirit—not a brute strength but a glorious inner strength—that Christ will live in you as you open the door and invite him in. And I ask him that with both feet planted firmly on love, you'll be able to take in with all followers of Jesus the extravagant dimensions of Christ's love. Reach out and experience the breadth! Test its length! Plumb the depths! Rise to the heights! Live full lives, full in the fullness of God."

PRAYER:

Magnificent Father, I ask in the name of Jesus Christ, that You strengthen me by Your Spirit—not a brute strength but a glorious inner strength—that Christ will live in me as I open the door and invite him in. That I will take in the extravagant dimensions of Christ's love and live a full life, in the fullness of God.

DAILY REFLECTION:

Take a moment to reflect on the Bible verse(s) for today and write your thoughts below:

BIBLE VERSE(S):

Hebrews 2:1-4 MSG

"It's crucial that we keep a firm grip on what we've heard so that we don't drift off. If the old message delivered by the angels was valid and nobody got away with anything, do you think we can risk neglecting this latest message, this magnificent salvation? First of all, it was delivered in person by the Master, then accurately passed on to us by those who heard it from him. All the while God was validating it with gifts through the Holy Spirit, all sorts of signs and miracles, as he saw fit."

PRAYER:

Father, in the name of Jesus Christ, I ask that the message of Your magnificent salvation continues to be passed on and validated with gifts through the Holy Spirit—all sorts of signs and miracles as You see fit.

DAILY REFLECTION:

Take a moment to reflect on the Bible verse(s) for today and write your thoughts below:

BIBLE VERSE(S):

Isaiah 28:28-29 NIV

"Grain must be ground to make bread; so one does not go on threshing it forever. The wheels of a threshing cart may be rolled over it, but one does not use horses to grind grain. All this also comes from the Lord Almighty, whose plan is wonderful, whose wisdom is magnificent."

PRAYER:

Father, in the name of Jesus Christ, I thank You for Your magnificent wisdom that is at work in my life.

DAILY REFLECTION:

Take a moment to reflect on the Bible verse(s) for today and write your thoughts below:

May 20

BIBLE VERSE(S):

Numbers 14:19 NKJV

"In keeping with your magnificent, unfailing love, please pardon the sins of this people, just as you have forgiven them ever since they left Egypt."

PRAYER:

Father, in the name of Jesus Christ, I thank You that in keeping with your magnificent, unfailing love, you pardon all my sins.

DAILY REFLECTION:

Take a moment to reflect on the Bible verse(s) for today and write your thoughts below:

BIBLE VERSE(S):

Psalm 48:2 NKJV

"It is high and magnificent; the whole earth rejoices to see it! Mount Zion, the holy mountain, is the city of the great King!"

PRAYER:

Father, in the name of Jesus Christ, I rejoice to see the high and magnificent Mount Zion, the holy mountain, the city of the great King!

DAILY REFLECTION:

Take a moment to reflect on the Bible verse(s) for today and write your thoughts below:

May 22

BIBLE VERSE(S):

Isaiah 63:14 NKJV

"As with cattle going down into a peaceful valley, the Spirit of the Lord gave them rest. You led your people, Lord, and gained a magnificent reputation."

PRAYER:

Magnificent God, Thank You for leading me and giving me rest.

DAILY REFLECTION:

Take a moment to reflect on the Bible verse(s) for today and write your thoughts below:

BIBLE VERSE(S):

Exodus 15:6 The Voice

"Your right hand, Eternal One, is magnificent in power. Your right hand, Eternal, vanquishes the enemy."

PRAYER:

I declare that the right hand of the Lord is magnificent in power in my life and vanquishes the enemy in the name of Jesus Christ.

DAILY REFLECTION:

Take a moment to reflect on the Bible verse(s) for today and write your thoughts below:

BIBLE VERSE(S):

1 Chronicles 16:29 The Voice

"Credit Him with the glory worthy of His magnificent name; gather your sacrifice, and present it before Him. Bow down to the Eternal, adorned in holiness."

PRAYER:

Father, in the name of Jesus Christ, I give You the credit worthy of Your magnificent name.

DAILY REFLECTION:

Take a moment to reflect on the Bible verse(s) for today and write your thoughts below:

BIBLE VERSE(S):

Psalm 145:3 MSG

"GOD is magnificent; he can never be praised enough. There are no boundaries to his greatness."

PRAYER:

Father, in the name of Jesus Christ, I declare that You are magnificent; You can never be praised enough. There are no boundaries to Your greatness. Thank You, Lord.

DAILY REFLECTION:

Take a moment to reflect on the Bible verse(s) for today and write your thoughts below:

BIBLE VERSE(S):

Genesis 45:7 AMP

"God sent me [to Egypt] ahead of you to preserve for you a remnant on the earth, and to keep you alive by a great escape."

PRAYER:

Father, in the name of Jesus, I decree and declare that You preserve me and keep me alive by great escapes.

DAILY REFLECTION:

Take a moment to reflect on the Bible verse(s) for today and write your thoughts below:

BIBLE VERSE(S):

2 Samuel 22:51 NIV

"He gives his king great victories; he shows unfailing kindness to his anointed, to David and his descendants forever."

PRAYER:

Father, in the name of Jesus, I decree and declare that You give me great victories and show unfailing kindness to me, to my family and to my descendants forever.

DAILY REFLECTION:

Take a moment to reflect on the Bible verse(s) for today and write your thoughts below:

May 28

BIBLE VERSE(S):

1 Chronicles 29:11 AMP

"Yours, O Lord, is the greatness and the power and the glory and the victory and the majesty, indeed everything that is in the heavens and on the earth; Yours is the dominion and kingdom, O Lord, and You exalt Yourself as head over all."

PRAYER:

Father, in the name of Jesus, I decree and declare that You are great, mighty, majestic, magnificent, glorious, and sovereign over all the heavens and on the earth. As You have dominion and exalt yourself as the head over all, I decree and declare that You rule over my life, in the name of Jesus Christ.

DAILY REFLECTION:

Take a moment to reflect on the Bible verse(s) for today and write your thoughts below:

BIBLE VERSE(S):

Isaiah 12:5 TLB

"Sing to the Lord, for he has done wonderful things. Make known his praise around the world."

PRAYER:

Father, in the name of Jesus Christ, I sing to You, for You have done wonderful things in my life and I will make known Your praise around the world.

DAILY REFLECTION:

Take a moment to reflect on the Bible verse(s) for today and write your thoughts below:

BIBLE VERSE(S):

Psalm 104:1 NIV

"Praise the Lord, my soul. Lord my God, you are very great; you are clothed with splendor and majesty."

PRAYER:

Father, in the name of Jesus, I praise You, O Lord my God, for You are magnificent. You are very great; you are clothed with splendor and majesty.

DAILY REFLECTION:

Take a moment to reflect on the Bible verse(s) for today and write your thoughts below:

May 31

BIBLE VERSE(S):

Psalm 136:4 NLT

"Give thanks to him who alone does mighty miracles. His faithful love endures forever."

PRAYER:

Father, in the name of Jesus Christ, I ask that You do mighty miracles in my life. I thank You, Lord, for Your faithful love endures forever.

DAILY REFLECTION:

Take a moment to reflect on the Bible verse(s) for today and write your thoughts below:

Father, in the name of Jesus, let our joy be limitless in the month of June and beyond as we receive all that we ask for in Jesus name. Amen.

CHAPTER 6
Joyous June

Until now you've not been bold enough to ask the Father for a single thing in my (JESUS) name, but now you can ask, and keep on asking him! And you can be sure that you'll receive what you ask for, and your joy will have no limits!
John 16:24 TPT

Welcome to Joyous June!

I hope you are ready to experience another level of joy—not as the world gives, but as God gives.

I pray that the Lord will bless you with unending joy and that as you experience the limitless joy of the Lord you will also experience His supernatural strength.

June 1

BIBLE VERSE(S):

Nehemiah 8:10 AMP

"Then Ezra said to them, "Go [your way], eat the rich festival food, drink the sweet drink, and send portions to him for whom nothing is prepared; for this day is holy to our Lord. And do not be worried, for the joy of the Lord is your strength and your stronghold."

PRAYER:

Father, in the name of Jesus Christ, I thank You for the start of a new month. I decree and declare that I will not be worried, for it is written in Nehemiah 8:10 that "the joy of the Lord is my strength and my stronghold."

DAILY REFLECTION:

Take a moment to reflect on the Bible verse(s) for today and write your thoughts below:

BIBLE VERSE(S):

1 Chronicles 13:8 AMP

"David and all Israel celebrated [joyfully] before God with all their might, with songs, lyres, harps, tambourines, cymbals, and trumpets."

PRAYER:

Father, in the name of Jesus Christ, I celebrate joyfully before You with all my might. I decree and declare that this month of June shall be full of joy, thus joyous for me.

DAILY REFLECTION:

Take a moment to reflect on the Bible verse(s) for today and write your thoughts below:

June 3

BIBLE VERSE(S):

Job 8:19 AMP

"Behold, this is the joy of His way; And from out of the dust others will spring up and grow [to take his place]."

PRAYER:

Father, in the name of Jesus Christ, I thank You for the joy in Your way; that others will spring up and grow.

DAILY REFLECTION:

Take a moment to reflect on the Bible verse(s) for today and write your thoughts below:

BIBLE VERSE(S):

Job 33:26 AMP

"He will pray to God, and He shall be favorable to him, So that he looks at His face with joy; For God restores to man His righteousness [that is, his right standing with God—with its joys]."

PRAYER:

Father, in the name of Jesus Christ, as I pray to You Lord, please be favorable to me, so that I look at Your face with joy. For You restore to me Your righteousness.

DAILY REFLECTION:

Take a moment to reflect on the Bible verse(s) for today and write your thoughts below:

June 5

BIBLE VERSE(S):

Psalm 5:11 AMP

"But let all who take refuge and put their trust in You rejoice, Let them ever sing for joy; Because You cover and shelter them, Let those who love Your name be joyful and exult in You."

PRAYER:

Father, in the name of Jesus Christ, I rejoice as I take refuge and put my trust in You. Let me ever sing for joy because You cover and shelter me. Let me be joyful and exult in You.

DAILY REFLECTION:

Take a moment to reflect on the Bible verse(s) for today and write your thoughts below:

BIBLE VERSE(S):

Psalm 16:11 AMP

"You will show me the path of life; In Your presence is fullness of joy; In Your right hand there are pleasures forevermore."

PRAYER:

Lord, how I love Your presence. I am thankful for Your presence in my life. Father, in the name of Jesus Christ, I ask that I continue to enjoy the fullness of joy in Your presence and pleasures forevermore in Your right hand.

DAILY REFLECTION:

Take a moment to reflect on the Bible verse(s) for today and write your thoughts below:

June 7

BIBLE VERSE(S):

Psalm 19:8 AMP

"The precepts of the Lord are right, bringing joy to the heart; The commandment of the Lord is pure, enlightening the eyes."

PRAYER:

Father, in the name of Jesus Christ, let Your right precepts bring joy to my heart and enlighten my eyes.

DAILY REFLECTION:

Take a moment to reflect on the Bible verse(s) for today and write your thoughts below:

BIBLE VERSE(S):

Psalm 20:5 AMP

"We will sing joyously over your victory, And in the name of our God we will set up our banners. May the Lord fulfill all your petitions."

PRAYER:

Father, in the name of Jesus Christ, I decree and declare that I will sing joyously over my victory. I thank You Lord that You shall fulfill all my petitions.

DAILY REFLECTION:

Take a moment to reflect on the Bible verse(s) for today and write your thoughts below:

June 9

BIBLE VERSE(S):

Psalm 21:6 AMP

"For You make him most blessed [and a blessing] forever; You make him joyful with the joy of Your presence."

PRAYER:

Father, in the name of Jesus Christ, I thank You for making me most blessed, and a blessing, forever; You make me joyful with the joy of Your presence.

DAILY REFLECTION:

Take a moment to reflect on the Bible verse(s) for today and write your thoughts below:

BIBLE VERSE(S):

Psalm 27:6 AMP

"And now my head will be lifted up above my enemies around me, In His tent I will offer sacrifices with shouts of joy; I will sing, yes, I will sing praises to the Lord."

PRAYER:

Father, in the name of Jesus Christ, I thank You for lifting my head up above my enemies around me; I will shout for joy and l will sing praises to the Lord

DAILY REFLECTION:

Take a moment to reflect on the Bible verse(s) for today and write your thoughts below:

BIBLE VERSE(S):

Psalm 30:5 AMP

"For His anger is but for a moment, His favor is for a lifetime. Weeping may endure for a night, But a shout of joy comes in the morning."

PRAYER:

Father, in the name of Jesus Christ, I thank You for the assurance of the certainty that joy comes in the morning.

DAILY REFLECTION:

Take a moment to reflect on the Bible verse(s) for today and write your thoughts below:

BIBLE VERSE(S):

Psalm 30:11 AMP

"You have turned my mourning into dancing for me; You have taken off my sackcloth and clothed me with joy,"

PRAYER:

Father, in the name of Jesus Christ, I thank You for taking off my sackcloth and clothing me with joy.

DAILY REFLECTION:

Take a moment to reflect on the Bible verse(s) for today and write your thoughts below:

June 13

BIBLE VERSE(S):

Psalm 35:27 AMP

"Let them shout for joy and rejoice, who favor my vindication and want what is right for me; Let them say continually, 'Let the Lord be magnified, who delights and takes pleasure in the prosperity of His servant.'"

PRAYER:

Father, in the name of Jesus Christ, let those who favor my vindication and want what is right for me shout for joy and rejoice. Let them say continually, "Let the Lord be magnified, who delights and takes pleasure in the prosperity of His servant."

DAILY REFLECTION:

Take a moment to reflect on the Bible verse(s) for today and write your thoughts below:

June 14

BIBLE VERSE(S):

Psalm 51:12 AMP

"Restore to me the joy of Your salvation And sustain me with a willing spirit."

PRAYER:

Father, in the name of Jesus Christ, I ask that You restore to me the joy of my salvation.

DAILY REFLECTION:

Take a moment to reflect on the Bible verse(s) for today and write your thoughts below:

June 15

BIBLE VERSE(S):

Psalm 9:1-2 MSG

"I'm thanking you, God, from a full heart, I'm writing the book on your wonders. I'm whistling, laughing, and jumping for joy; I'm singing your song, High God."

PRAYER:

Father, in the name of Jesus Christ, I thank You, God, from a full heart, I'm writing the book on your wonders. I'm whistling, laughing, and jumping for joy; I'm singing your song, High God

DAILY REFLECTION:

Take a moment to reflect on the Bible verse(s) for today and write your thoughts below:

June 16

BIBLE VERSE(S):

Psalm 19:7-9 MSG

"The revelation of God is whole and pulls our lives together. The signposts of God are clear and point out the right road. The life-maps of God are right, showing the way to joy. The directions of God are plain and easy on the eyes. God's reputation is twenty-four-carat gold, with a lifetime guarantee. The decisions of God are accurate down to the nth degree."

PRAYER:

Father, in the name of Jesus Christ, I ask that You pull my life together through Your revelation. I receive Your clear signposts that point out the right road for me. I receive life-maps from You, showing me the way of joy.

DAILY REFLECTION:

Take a moment to reflect on the Bible verse(s) for today and write your thoughts below:

BIBLE VERSE(S):

Psalm 28:6-7 MSG

"Blessed be God— he heard me praying. He proved he's on my side; I've thrown my lot in with him. Now I'm jumping for joy, and shouting and singing my thanks to him."

PRAYER:

Father, in the name of Jesus Christ, I declare that You are blessed, for You heard me praying and You proved You're on my side. Now I'm jumping for joy, and shouting and singing my thanks to You.

DAILY REFLECTION:

Take a moment to reflect on the Bible verse(s) for today and write your thoughts below:

BIBLE VERSE(S):

Psalm 33:20-22 MSG

“We’re depending on God; he’s everything we need. What’s more, our hearts brim with joy since we’ve taken for our own his holy name. Love us, God, with all you’ve got— that’s what we’re depending on.”

PRAYER:

Father, I depend on you; You are everything I need. My heart brims with joy since I’ve taken for my own Your holy name. Thank You for loving me, God, as that’s what I’m depending on, in the name of Jesus Christ.

DAILY REFLECTION:

Take a moment to reflect on the Bible verse(s) for today and write your thoughts below:

June 19

BIBLE VERSE(S):

Psalm 68:1-4 MSG

"Up with God! Down with his enemies! Adversaries, run for the hills! Gone like a puff of smoke, like a blob of wax in the fire— one look at God and the wicked vanish. When the righteous see God in action they'll laugh, they'll sing, they'll laugh and sing for joy. Sing hymns to God; all heaven, sing out; clear the way for the coming of Cloud-Rider. Enjoy God, cheer when you see him!"

PRAYER:

Father, in the name of Jesus Christ, I decree and declare that I shall see You in action in my life, and I'll laugh, I'll sing, I'll laugh and sing for joy. I will enjoy God and cheer when I see Him doing wonderful things in and around my life in the name of Jesus Christ.

DAILY REFLECTION:

Take a moment to reflect on the Bible verse(s) for today and write your thoughts below:

BIBLE VERSE(S):

Psalm 92:4-9 MSG

"You made me so happy, God. I saw your work and I shouted for joy. How magnificent your work, God! How profound your thoughts! Dullards never notice what you do; fools never do get it. When the wicked popped up like weeds and all the evil men and women took over, You mowed them down, finished them off once and for all. You, God, are High and Eternal. Look at your enemies, God! Look at your enemies—ruined! Scattered to the winds, all those hirelings of evil!"

Today's Bible verse is very thought provoking. I find it fascinating that even though the works of God are magnificent, it is amazing that some people do not notice or understand what God does. Let us pray that everyone will, at some point in their life, come to realize how great God is so that their belief is established and set in stone through their own personal encounter with God and not just by what they hear about God.

PRAYER:

Father, in the name of Jesus, I thank You because You make me so happy, God. I continue to see your work and I will continue to shout for joy. How magnificent your work, God!

DAILY REFLECTION:

Take a moment to reflect on the Bible verse(s) for today and write your thoughts below:

June 21

BIBLE VERSE(S):

Galatians 5:22 NLT

"But the Holy Spirit produces this kind of fruit in our lives: love, joy, peace, patience, kindness, goodness, faithfulness,"

PRAYER:

Father in the name of Jesus Christ, I thank You that the Holy Spirit produces the fruit of joy in my life in addition to love, peace, patience, kindness, goodness, and faithfulness.

DAILY REFLECTION:

Take a moment to reflect on the Bible verse(s) for today and write your thoughts below:

BIBLE VERSE(S):

Psalm 21:6 NLT

"You have endowed him with eternal blessings and given him the joy of your presence."

PRAYER:

Father, in the name of Jesus Christ, I thank You for endowing me with eternal blessings and giving me the joy of Your presence.

DAILY REFLECTION:

Take a moment to reflect on the Bible verse(s) for today and write your thoughts below:

BIBLE VERSE(S):

Psalm 28:7 NLT

"The Lord is my strength and shield. I trust him with all my heart. He helps me, and my heart is filled with joy. I burst out in songs of thanksgiving."

PRAYER:

Father, in the name of Jesus Christ, I decree and declare that You are my strength and shield. I trust You with all my heart. You help me and my heart is filled with joy.

DAILY REFLECTION:

Take a moment to reflect on the Bible verse(s) for today and write your thoughts below:

BIBLE VERSE(S):

Psalm 34:5 NLT

"Those who look to him for help will be radiant with joy; no shadow of shame will darken their faces."

PRAYER:

Father, in the name of Jesus Christ, I decree and declare that as I look to You for help, I will be radiant with joy and no shame will darken my face.

DAILY REFLECTION:

Take a moment to reflect on the Bible verse(s) for today and write your thoughts below:

BIBLE VERSE(S):

Psalm 43:4 NLT

"There I will go to the altar of God, to God—the source of all my joy. I will praise you with my harp, O God, my God!"

PRAYER:

Father, in the name of Jesus Christ, I go to Your altar, to You my God—the source of all my joy. I will praise You, O God, my God!

DAILY REFLECTION:

Take a moment to reflect on the Bible verse(s) for today and write your thoughts below:

BIBLE VERSE(S):

Psalm 63:7 NLT

"Because you are my helper, I sing for joy in the shadow of your wings."

PRAYER:

Father, in the name of Jesus Christ, I declare that You are my helper and I sing for joy in the shadow of Your wings.

DAILY REFLECTION:

Take a moment to reflect on the Bible verse(s) for today and write your thoughts below:

BIBLE VERSE(S):

Psalm 70:4 NLT

"But may all who search for you be filled with joy and gladness in you. May those who love your salvation repeatedly shout, 'God is great!'"

PRAYER:

Father, in the name of Jesus Christ, I ask that You fill me with joy and gladness in You as I search for You.

DAILY REFLECTION:

Take a moment to reflect on the Bible verse(s) for today and write your thoughts below:

June 28

BIBLE VERSE(S):

Psalm 92:4 NLT

"You thrill me, Lord, with all you have done for me! I sing for joy because of what you have done."

PRAYER:

Father, in the name of Jesus Christ, I thank You for all You have done for me. You thrill me, Lord, with all you have done for me. I sing for joy because of what You have done.

DAILY REFLECTION:

Take a moment to reflect on the Bible verse(s) for today and write your thoughts below:

BIBLE VERSE(S):

Psalm 128:2 NLT

"You will enjoy the fruit of your labor. How joyful and prosperous you will be!"

PRAYER:

Father, in the name of Jesus Christ, I decree and declare that I will enjoy the fruit of my labor. I will be joyful and prosperous.

DAILY REFLECTION:

Take a moment to reflect on the Bible verse(s) for today and write your thoughts below:

June 30

BIBLE VERSE(S):

Psalm 145:7 NLT

"Everyone will share the story of your wonderful goodness; they will sing with joy about your righteousness."

PRAYER:

Father, in the name of Jesus Christ, I decree and declare that I will share the story of Your wonderful goodness. I will sing for joy about Your righteousness.

DAILY REFLECTION:

Take a moment to reflect on the Bible verse(s) for today and write your thoughts below:

Father, in the name of Jesus, give us many reasons to shout for joy in the month of July.

CHAPTER 7

Jubilant July

Shout for joy to the Lord, all the earth, burst into jubilant song with music.
Psalm 98:4 NIV

Welcome to Jubilant July!

Praise The Lord! Hallelujah! Hallelujah! Hallelujah!

This month, I pray that you will be intentional about rejoicing, jubilating, and praising God. At least for the gift of life and the fact that you made through to half of the year. These are worthwhile reasons to jubilate, rejoice, sing, dance. and give God praise. As you do so, may the Lord bless you with many more reasons to rejoice and be jubilant in the precious name of Jesus Christ.

July 1

BIBLE VERSE(S):

Isaiah 44:23 AMP

"Shout for joy, O heavens, for the Lord has done it! Shout in triumph, you depths of the earth; Break forth into jubilant rejoicing, you mountains, O forest, and every tree in it! For the Lord has redeemed Jacob, And He shows His glory in Israel."

PRAYER:

Father, in the name of Jesus Christ, I thank You for a jubilant July! I decree and declare that I shall break forth into jubilant rejoicing. For the Lord has redeemed me and He shows His glory in my life.

DAILY REFLECTION:

Take a moment to reflect on the Bible verse(s) for today and write your thoughts below:

BIBLE VERSE(S):

Psalm 98:4 NIV

"Shout for joy to the Lord, all the earth, burst into jubilant song with music..."

PRAYER:

Father in the name of Jesus Christ, I burst into jubilant song with music. I shout for joy to the Lord. Hallelujah!

DAILY REFLECTION:

Take a moment to reflect on the Bible verse(s) for today and write your thoughts below:

BIBLE VERSE(S):

1 Chronicles 16:30-33 MSG

"God is serious business, take him seriously; he's put the earth in place and it's not moving. So let Heaven rejoice, let Earth be jubilant, and pass the word among the nations, 'God reigns!' Let Ocean, all teeming with life, bellow, let Field and all its creatures shake the rafters; Then the trees in the forest will add their applause to all who are pleased and present before God —he's on his way to set things right!"

PRAYER:

Father, in the name of Jesus Christ, I declare that I shall be jubilant for, God, You reign! You are on Your way to set things right.

DAILY REFLECTION:

Take a moment to reflect on the Bible verse(s) for today and write your thoughts below:

BIBLE VERSE(S):

Psalm 68:3 ESV

"But the righteous shall be glad; they shall exult before God; they shall be jubilant with joy!"

PRAYER:

Father, in the name of Jesus Christ, today, I declare that I shall be glad and glory before You. I shall jubilantly rejoice with joy!

DAILY REFLECTION:

Take a moment to reflect on the Bible verse(s) for today and write your thoughts below:

BIBLE VERSE(S):

Jeremiah 31:12 AMP

"They will come and sing aloud and shout for joy on the height of Zion, And will be radiant [with joy] over the goodness of the Lord— For the grain, for the new wine, for the oil, And for the young of the flock and the herd. And their life will be like a watered garden, And they shall never sorrow or languish again."

PRAYER:

Father, in the name of Jesus Christ, I decree and declare that I shall be jubilant over Your goodness in my life. My life will be like a watered garden, and I shall never sorrow or languish again.

DAILY REFLECTION:

Take a moment to reflect on the Bible verse(s) for today and write your thoughts below:

BIBLE VERSE(S):

Psalms 33:3 NIV

"Sing to him a new song; play skillfully, and shout for joy."

PRAYER:

Father, in the name of Jesus Christ, I decree and declare that I shall sing a new song to the Lord and jubilantly shout for joy.

DAILY REFLECTION:

Take a moment to reflect on the Bible verse(s) for today and write your thoughts below:

BIBLE VERSE(S):

Psalm 47:1 HCSB

"Clap your hands, all you peoples; shout to God with a jubilant cry."

PRAYER:

Father, in the name of Jesus Christ, today I clap my hands and shout to You, my God, with a jubilant cry.

DAILY REFLECTION:

Take a moment to reflect on the Bible verse(s) for today and write your thoughts below:

BIBLE VERSE(S):

Psalm 68:4 NLT

"Sing praises to God and to his name! Sing loud praises to him who rides the clouds. His name is the Lord—rejoice in his presence!"

PRAYER:

Father, in the name of Jesus Christ, I sing praises to You and Your name. I am jubilant in Your presence.

DAILY REFLECTION:

Take a moment to reflect on the Bible verse(s) for today and write your thoughts below:

BIBLE VERSE(S):

Psalm 98:4 HCSB

"Shout to the Lord, all the earth; be jubilant, shout for joy, and sing."

PRAYER:

Father, in the name of Jesus Christ, I declare that I shall be jubilant, shout for joy, and sing to You, Lord.

DAILY REFLECTION:

Take a moment to reflect on the Bible verse(s) for today and write your thoughts below:

BIBLE VERSE(S):

Jeremiah 25:30 AMP

"Therefore prophesy all these words against them and say to them: 'The Lord will roar from on high And utter His voice from His holy dwelling; He will roar mightily against His fold and pasture. He will jubilantly shout like those who tread the grapes [in the wine press], Against all the inhabitants of the earth."

PRAYER:

Father, in the name of Jesus Christ, I ask that You roar from on high, from Your holy dwelling place, and that You give a jubilant shout!

DAILY REFLECTION:

Take a moment to reflect on the Bible verse(s) for today and write your thoughts below:

BIBLE VERSE(S):

Jeremiah 50:11 NASB

"Because you are glad, because you are jubilant, O you who pillage My heritage, Because you skip about like a threshing heifer And neigh like stallions,"

PRAYER:

Father, in the name of Jesus Christ, I declare that I am glad and I am jubilant and skip about like a threshing heifer and neigh like stallions.

DAILY REFLECTION:

Take a moment to reflect on the Bible verse(s) for today and write your thoughts below:

BIBLE VERSE(S):

Zephaniah 3:14 AMP

"Shout for joy, O Daughter of Zion! Shout in triumph, O Israel! Rejoice, be in high spirits and glory with all your heart, O Daughter of Jerusalem [in that day]!"

PRAYER:

Father, in the name of Jesus Christ, I decree and declare that I shall shout for joy, and I shout in triumph today. I will rejoice and be jubilant with all my heart.

DAILY REFLECTION:

Take a moment to reflect on the Bible verse(s) for today and write your thoughts below:

July 13

BIBLE VERSE(S):

1 Chronicles 16:8-19 MSG

"Thank God! Call out his Name! Tell the whole world who he is and what he's done! Sing to him! Play songs for him! Broadcast all his wonders! Revel in his holy Name, God-seekers, be jubilant! Study God and his strength, seek his presence day and night; Remember all the wonders he performed, the miracles and judgments that came out of his mouth. Seed of Israel his servant! Children of Jacob, his first choice! He is God, our God; wherever you go you come on his judgments and decisions. He keeps his commitments across thousands of generations, the covenant he commanded, The same one he made with Abraham, the very one he swore to Isaac; He posted it in big block letters to Jacob, this eternal covenant with Israel: 'I give you the land of Canaan, this is your inheritance; Even though you're not much to look at, a few straggling strangers.'"

PRAYER:

Thank You, Heavenly Father, Jehovah! I shall tell the whole world who You are and what You've done! I sing to You! I play songs for You! I broadcast all Your wonders! I revel in Your holy Name, as a God-seekers, I am jubilant!

DAILY REFLECTION:

Take a moment to reflect on the Bible verse(s) for today

and write your thoughts below:

BIBLE VERSE(S):

Zechariah 9:9 The Voice

"Cry out with joy, O daughter of Zion! Shout jubilantly, O daughter of Jerusalem! Look—your King is coming; He is righteous and able to save. He comes seated humbly on a donkey, on a colt, a foal of a donkey."

PRAYER:

Today, I shall shout jubilantly! For my King Jesus Christ is coming. He is righteous and able to save. Hallelujah!

DAILY REFLECTION:

Take a moment to reflect on the Bible verse(s) for today and write your thoughts below:

BIBLE VERSE(S):

1 Thessalonians 3:9 The Voice

"What thanks would ever be enough to offer God about you for all the jubilant celebration we'll feel before our God because of you?"

PRAYER:

Father, in the name of Jesus Christ, I offer You thanks for the jubilant celebration I will feel before You my God.

DAILY REFLECTION:

Take a moment to reflect on the Bible verse(s) for today and write your thoughts below:

BIBLE VERSE(S):

Luke 7:16 The Voice

"and everyone was both shocked and jubilant. They praised God. Funeral Crowd: A tremendous prophet has arisen in our midst! God has visited His people!"

PRAYER:

Father, in the name of Jesus Christ, I ask that You do something great in my life that everyone who hears about it will be shocked and jubilant.

DAILY REFLECTION:

Take a moment to reflect on the Bible verse(s) for today and write your thoughts below:

BIBLE VERSE(S):

1 Chronicles 16:32 NIV

"Let the sea resound, and all that is in it; let the fields be jubilant, and everything in them!"

PRAYER:

Father, in the name of Jesus Christ, I decree and declare let there be all around a jubilant celebration for me.

DAILY REFLECTION:

Take a moment to reflect on the Bible verse(s) for today and write your thoughts below:

July 18

BIBLE VERSE(S):

Psalm 96:12 NIV

"Let the fields be jubilant, and everything in them; let all the trees of the forest sing for joy."

PRAYER:

Father, in the name of Jesus Christ, I decree that I shall be jubilant just as the fields and I will sing for joy like the trees of the forest.

DAILY REFLECTION:

Take a moment to reflect on the Bible verse(s) for today and write your thoughts below:

BIBLE VERSE(S):

Psalm 40:16 NLT

"But may all who search for you be filled with joy and gladness in you. May those who love your salvation repeatedly shout, 'The Lord is great!'"

PRAYER:

Father, in the name of Jesus Christ, I decree and declare that as I search for You, I shall be filled with joy and gladness in You. I shall jubilantly shout "The Lord is great!"

DAILY REFLECTION:

Take a moment to reflect on the Bible verse(s) for today and write your thoughts below:

July 20

BIBLE VERSE(S):

2 Chronicles 15:14 AMP

"They swore an oath to the Lord with a loud voice, with [jubilant] shouting, with trumpets, and with horns."

PRAYER:

Father, in the name of Jesus Christ, I decree and declare that my jubilant shouting shall be done with a loud voice.

DAILY REFLECTION:

Take a moment to reflect on the Bible verse(s) for today and write your thoughts below:

BIBLE VERSE(S):

Isaiah 44:23 AMP

"Shout for joy, O heavens, for the Lord has done it! Shout in triumph, you depths of the earth; Break forth into jubilant rejoicing, you mountains, O forest, and every tree in it! For the Lord has redeemed Jacob, And He shows His glory in Israel."

PRAYER:

Father, in the name of Jesus Christ, I decree and declare that I shall shout for joy, for the Lord has done it! I shall shout in triumph and break forth into jubilant rejoicing for the Lord has redeemed me and He shows His glory in my life.

DAILY REFLECTION:

Take a moment to reflect on the Bible verse(s) for today and write your thoughts below:

BIBLE VERSE(S):

2 Samuel 6:12 NLT

"Then King David was told, 'The Lord has blessed Obed-edom's household and everything he has because of the Ark of God.' So David went there and brought the Ark of God from the house of Obed-edom to the City of David with a great celebration."

PRAYER:

Father, in the name of Jesus Christ, I decree and declare that just as You blessed the household of Obed-Edom, you shall bless my household and we shall praise You with jubilation.

DAILY REFLECTION:

Take a moment to reflect on the Bible verse(s) for today and write your thoughts below:

BIBLE VERSE(S):

Jeremiah 15:16 AMP

"Your words were found and I ate them, And Your words became a joy to me and the delight of my heart; For I have been called by Your name, O Lord God of hosts."

PRAYER:

Father, in the name of Jesus Christ, as I continue to find Your words and I eat them, Your words shall become a joy and jubilation to me and the delight of my heart, for I have been called by Your name, O Lord God of hosts.

DAILY REFLECTION:

Take a moment to reflect on the Bible verse(s) for today and write your thoughts below:

___

___

___

___

___

___

___

___

___

___

BIBLE VERSE(S):

Jeremiah 33:11 NLT

"...the sounds of joy and laughter. The joyful voices of bridegrooms and brides will be heard again, along with the joyous songs of people bringing thanksgiving offerings to the Lord. They will sing, 'Give thanks to the Lord of Heaven's Armies, for the Lord is good. His faithful love endures forever!' For I will restore the prosperity of this land to what it was in the past, says the Lord."

PRAYER:

Father, in the name of Jesus Christ, today I praise You with a voice of jubilation and a voice of joy for You are the Lord of Heaven's Armies, for You are good, and Your faithful love endures forever.

DAILY REFLECTION:

Take a moment to reflect on the Bible verse(s) for today and write your thoughts below:

BIBLE VERSE(S):

Isaiah 13:3 NIV

"I have commanded those I prepared for battle; I have summoned my warriors to carry out my wrath - those who rejoice in my triumph."

PRAYER:

Father, in the name of Jesus Christ, I decree and declare that I obey Your command and I jubilantly rejoice in Your triumph.

DAILY REFLECTION:

Take a moment to reflect on the Bible verse(s) for today and write your thoughts below:

BIBLE VERSE(S):

Luke 10:17 CJB

"The seventy came back jubilant. 'Lord,' they said, 'with your power, even the demons submit to us!'"

PRAYER:

Father, in the name of Jesus Christ, I decree and declare that I come back jubilant to You for with Your power, demons always submit to me.

DAILY REFLECTION:

Take a moment to reflect on the Bible verse(s) for today and write your thoughts below:

BIBLE VERSE(S):

1 Chronicles 16:32 EXB

"Let the sea and everything in it ·shout [roar; thunder]; let the fields and everything in them ·rejoice [exult; celebrate; be jubilant]."

PRAYER:

Father, in the name of Jesus Christ, I decree and declare that I shall shout, rejoice, celebrate, and be jubilant.

DAILY REFLECTION:

Take a moment to reflect on the Bible verse(s) for today and write your thoughts below:

July 28

BIBLE VERSE(S):

Psalms 92:4-5 MSG

"You made me so happy, God. I saw your work and I shouted for joy. How magnificent your work, God! How profound your thoughts!"

PRAYER:

Father, in the name of Jesus Christ, I decree and declare that You make me jubilant by your magnificent works. I shout for joy at the works of Your hands.

DAILY REFLECTION:

Take a moment to reflect on the Bible verse(s) for today and write your thoughts below:

BIBLE VERSE(S):

2 Chronicles 20:22 NIV

"As they began to sing and praise, the Lord set ambushes against the men of Ammon and Moab and Mount Seir who were invading Judah, and they were defeated."

PRAYER:

Father, in the name of Jesus Christ, I thank You because at the moment I begin my jubilant praise to You, You will set ambushes against all evil and defeat them.

DAILY REFLECTION:

Take a moment to reflect on the Bible verse(s) for today and write your thoughts below:

BIBLE VERSE(S):

Psalm 9:2 NASB

"I will rejoice and be jubilant in You; I will sing praise to Your name, O Most High."

PRAYER:

Father, in the name of Jesus Christ, I decree and declare that I will rejoice and be jubilant in You; I will sing praise to Your name, O Most High.

DAILY REFLECTION:

Take a moment to reflect on the Bible verse(s) for today and write your thoughts below:

BIBLE VERSE(S):

Psalm 70:5 TLB

"But may the joy of the Lord be given to everyone who loves him and his salvation. May they constantly exclaim, 'How great God is!'"

PRAYER:

Father, in the name of Jesus Christ, I decree and declare that the joy of the Lord shall be given to me, and I shall constantly exclaim with jubilee, "How great God is!"

DAILY REFLECTION:

Take a moment to reflect on the Bible verse(s) for today and write your thoughts below:

Father, I ask that You perform awesome miracles for us in the month of August and beyond in Jesus name.

CHAPTER 8

Awesome August

Come and see what our God has done, what awesome miracles he performs for people!
Psalms 66:5 NLT

Welcome to Awesome August!

In this month of August, my prayer is that you will see and experience how awesome God is.

I pray that you will praise God for He is awesome in all His ways and all that He does.

Take some time to reflect on the awesome nature of God as recorded in the Bible verses for this month. Believe and expect that God will do awesome things with you and in your life for He is the same God yesterday, today and forever.

August 1

BIBLE VERSE(S):

Exodus 15:11 AMP

"Who is like You among the gods, O Lord? Who is like You, majestic in holiness, Awesome in splendor, working wonders?"

PRAYER:

Father, in the name of Jesus Christ, I declare that there is no one like You among the gods. There is no one like You who is majestic in holiness, awesome in splendor, and working wonders. Hallelujah!

DAILY REFLECTION:

Take a moment to reflect on the Bible verse(s) for today and write your thoughts below:

August 2

BIBLE VERSE(S):

Exodus 34:10 AMP

"Then God said, 'Behold, I am going to make a covenant. Before all your people I will do wondrous works (miracles) such as have not been created or produced in all the earth nor among any of the nations; and all the people among whom you live shall see the working of the Lord, for it is a fearful and awesome thing that I am going to do with you.'"

PRAYER:

Father, in the name of Jesus Christ, I decree and declare over my life that You will do wondrous works (miracles) such as have not been created or produced in all the earth nor among any of the nations, for it is a fearful and awesome thing that You are going to do with me.

DAILY REFLECTION:

Take a moment to reflect on the Bible verse(s) for today and write your thoughts below:

August 3

BIBLE VERSE(S):

Deuteronomy 7:21 AMP

"You shall not dread them, for the Lord your God is in your midst, a great and awesome God."

PRAYER:

Father, in the name of Jesus Christ, I decree and declare that I shall not dread anyone, for the Lord my God is in my midst, a great and awesome God.

DAILY REFLECTION:

Take a moment to reflect on the Bible verse(s) for today and write your thoughts below:

BIBLE VERSE(S):

Deuteronomy 10:17 AMP

"For the Lord your God is the God of gods and the Lord of lords, the great, the mighty, the awesome God who does not show partiality nor take a bribe."

PRAYER:

Father, in the name of Jesus Christ, I praise You for You are the Lord my God, God of gods, and the Lord of lords, the great, the mighty, the awesome God who does not show partiality nor take a bribe.

DAILY REFLECTION:

Take a moment to reflect on the Bible verse(s) for today and write your thoughts below:

BIBLE VERSE(S):

Deuteronomy 10:21 AMP

"He is your praise and glory; He is your God, who has done for you these great and awesome things which you have seen with your own eyes."

PRAYER:

Father, in the name of Jesus Christ, I thank You for You are my praise and glory; You are my God, who has done for me great and awesome things which I have seen with your own eyes.

DAILY REFLECTION:

Take a moment to reflect on the Bible verse(s) for today and write your thoughts below:

BIBLE VERSE(S):

Nehemiah 4:14 AMP

"When I saw their fear, I stood and said to the nobles and officials and the rest of the people: 'Do not be afraid of them; [confidently] remember the Lord who is great and awesome, and [with courage from Him] fight for your brothers, your sons, your daughters, your wives, and for your homes.'"

PRAYER:

Father, in the name of Jesus Christ, I decree and declare that I confidently remember You, my Lord who is great and awesome, and with courage from You, Lord, I fight for my family and for my home.

DAILY REFLECTION:

Take a moment to reflect on the Bible verse(s) for today and write your thoughts below:

August 7

BIBLE VERSE(S):

Psalm 65:5 AMP

"By awesome and wondrous things You answer us in righteousness, O God of our salvation, You who are the trust and hope of all the ends of the earth and of the farthest sea..."

PRAYER:

Father, in the name of Jesus Christ, I thank You that by awesome and wondrous things You answer me in righteousness, O God of my salvation, You who are the trust and hope of all the ends of the earth and of the farthest sea.

DAILY REFLECTION:

Take a moment to reflect on the Bible verse(s) for today and write your thoughts below:

August 8

BIBLE VERSE(S):

Psalm 66:5 AMP

"Come and see the works of God, He is awesome in His deeds toward the children of men."

PRAYER:

Father, in the name of Jesus Christ, I decree and declare that all shall come and see the works of God in my life, for He is awesome in His deeds towards me.

DAILY REFLECTION:

Take a moment to reflect on the Bible verse(s) for today and write your thoughts below:

August 9

BIBLE VERSE(S):

Psalm 68:35 AMP

"O God, You are awesome and profoundly majestic from Your sanctuary; The God of Israel gives strength and power to His people. Blessed be God!"

PRAYER:

Father, in the name of Jesus Christ, I decree and declare that O God, You are awesome and profoundly majestic from Your sanctuary; The God of Israel Who gives strength and power to me. Blessed be God!

DAILY REFLECTION:

Take a moment to reflect on the Bible verse(s) for today and write your thoughts below:

BIBLE VERSE(S):

Psalm 77:14 AMP

"You are the [awesome] God who works [powerful] wonders; You have demonstrated Your power among the people."

PRAYER:

Father, in the name of Jesus Christ, I thank You because You are the awesome God who works powerful wonders. You have demonstrated Your power in my life.

DAILY REFLECTION:

Take a moment to reflect on the Bible verse(s) for today and write your thoughts below:

BIBLE VERSE(S):

Psalm 89:7 AMP

"A God greatly feared and reverently worshiped in the council of the holy [angelic] ones, And awesome above all those who are around Him?"

PRAYER:

Father, in the name of Jesus Christ, I decree and declare that You are God, greatly feared and reverently worshiped in the council of the holy [angelic] ones, and awesome above all those who are around You.

DAILY REFLECTION:

Take a moment to reflect on the Bible verse(s) for today and write your thoughts below:

August 12

BIBLE VERSE(S):

Psalm 99:3 AMP

"Let them [reverently] praise Your great and awesome name; Holy is He."

PRAYER:

Father, in the name of Jesus Christ, I praise Your great and awesome name; Holy are You, God.

DAILY REFLECTION:

Take a moment to reflect on the Bible verse(s) for today and write your thoughts below:

August 13

BIBLE VERSE(S):

Psalm 111:9 AMP

"He has sent redemption to His people; He has ordained His covenant forever; Holy and awesome is His name—[inspiring reverence and godly fear]."

PRAYER:

Father, in the name of Jesus Christ, I praise You for You are Holy and awesome is Your name. Jehovah! Almighty! Everlasting Father! Yahweh!

DAILY REFLECTION:

Take a moment to reflect on the Bible verse(s) for today and write your thoughts below:

BIBLE VERSE(S):

Psalm 145:6 AMP

"People will speak of the power of Your awesome acts, And [with gratitude and submissive wonder] I will tell of Your greatness."

PRAYER:

Father, in the name of Jesus Christ, I decree and declare that I will join people to speak of the power of Your awesome acts, and with gratitude and submissive wonder I will tell of Your greatness in my life.

DAILY REFLECTION:

Take a moment to reflect on the Bible verse(s) for today and write your thoughts below:

BIBLE VERSE(S):

Proverbs 2:5 AMP

"Then you will understand the [reverent] fear of the Lord [that is, worshiping Him and regarding Him as truly awesome] And discover the knowledge of God."

PRAYER:

Father, in the name of Jesus Christ, I ask that You cause me to understand the reverent fear of the Lord, to worship You and regard You as truly awesome, and discover the knowledge of God.

DAILY REFLECTION:

Take a moment to reflect on the Bible verse(s) for today and write your thoughts below:

August 16

BIBLE VERSE(S):

Isaiah 8:13 AMP

"It is the Lord of hosts whom you are to regard as holy and awesome. He shall be your [source of] fear, He shall be your [source of] dread [not man]."

PRAYER:

Father, in the name of Jesus Christ, I rise today to regard You alone as holy and awesome.

DAILY REFLECTION:

Take a moment to reflect on the Bible verse(s) for today and write your thoughts below:

August 17

BIBLE VERSE(S):

Daniel 9:4 AMP

"I prayed to the Lord my God and confessed and said, 'O Lord, the great and awesome God, who keeps His covenant and extends lovingkindness toward those who love Him and keep His commandments...'"

PRAYER:

Father, in the name of Jesus Christ, I decree and declare that You, O Lord, are the great and awesome God, who keeps His covenant and extends lovingkindness towards those who love Him and keep His commandments, including me.

DAILY REFLECTION:

Take a moment to reflect on the Bible verse(s) for today and write your thoughts below:

August 18

BIBLE VERSE(S):

Hebrews 1:3 AMP

"The Son is the radiance and only expression of the glory of [our awesome] God [reflecting God's Shekinah glory, the Light-being, the brilliant light of the divine], and the exact representation and perfect imprint of His [Father's] essence, and upholding and maintaining and propelling all things [the entire physical and spiritual universe] by His powerful word [carrying the universe along to its predetermined goal]. When He [Himself and no other] had [by offering Himself on the cross as a sacrifice for sin] accomplished purification from sins and established our freedom from guilt, He sat down [revealing His completed work] at the right hand of the Majesty on high [revealing His Divine authority],"

PRAYER:

Father, in the name of Jesus Christ, I thank You for the gift of Your precious Son, Jesus Christ, who is the radiance and only expression of Your glory, awesome God.

DAILY REFLECTION:

Take a moment to reflect on the Bible verse(s) for today and write your thoughts below:

___

___

___

August 19

BIBLE VERSE(S):

2 Samuel 7:23 NLT

"What other nation on earth is like your people Israel? What other nation, O God, have you redeemed from slavery to be your own people? You made a great name for yourself when you redeemed your people from Egypt. You performed awesome miracles and drove out the nations and gods that stood in their way."

PRAYER:

Father, in the name of Jesus Christ, I ask that You make a great name for Yourself in my life as You perform awesome miracles in my life and drive out the nations and gods that stand in my way.

DAILY REFLECTION:

Take a moment to reflect on the Bible verse(s) for today and write your thoughts below:

BIBLE VERSE(S):

Psalm 47:2 NLT

"For the Lord Most High is awesome. He is the great King of all the earth."

PRAYER:

Father, in the name of Jesus Christ, I decree and declare that You, the Lord Most High, are awesome, You are the great King of all the earth."

DAILY REFLECTION:

Take a moment to reflect on the Bible verse(s) for today and write your thoughts below:

August 21

BIBLE VERSE(S):

Psalm 66:3 NKJV

"Say to God, 'How awesome are Your works! Through the greatness of Your power Your enemies shall submit themselves to You.'"

PRAYER:

Father, in the name of Jesus Christ, I declare how awesome are Your works! Through the greatness of Your power Your enemies shall submit themselves to You. Hallelujah!

DAILY REFLECTION:

Take a moment to reflect on the Bible verse(s) for today and write your thoughts below:

BIBLE VERSE(S):

Psalm 76:11 NLT

"Make vows to the Lord your God, and keep them. Let everyone bring tribute to the Awesome One."

PRAYER:

Father, in the name of Jesus Christ, today I bring tributes to You as the Awesome One, the Only living God!

DAILY REFLECTION:

Take a moment to reflect on the Bible verse(s) for today and write your thoughts below:

August 23

BIBLE VERSE(S):

Psalm 99:3 NLT

"Let them praise your great and awesome name. Your name is holy!"

PRAYER:

Father, in the name of Jesus Christ, I praise Your great and awesome name. Your name is holy!

DAILY REFLECTION:

Take a moment to reflect on the Bible verse(s) for today and write your thoughts below:

BIBLE VERSE(S):

Nehemiah 1:5-6 MSG

"I said, 'God, God-of-Heaven, the great and awesome God, loyal to his covenant and faithful to those who love him and obey his commands: Look at me, listen to me. Pay attention to this prayer of your servant that I'm praying day and night in intercession for your servants, the People of Israel, confessing the sins of the People of Israel. And I'm including myself, I and my ancestors, among those who have sinned against you.'"

PRAYER:

Father God, God-of-Heaven, the great and awesome God, loyal to His covenant and faithful to those who love Him and obey His commands: I ask in the name of Jesus Christ, that You look at me, listen to me. Pay attention to this prayer that I'm praying day and night in intercession for my family and I, confessing our sins, I'm including myself and my ancestors, among those who have sinned against you. Father, I plead the blood of Jesus Christ over us and ask that You show us Your mercy, O great and awesome God.

DAILY REFLECTION:

Take a moment to reflect on the Bible verse(s) for today and write your thoughts below:

BIBLE VERSE(S):

Deuteronomy 6:22 WEB

"...and Yahweh showed great and awesome signs and wonders on Egypt, on Pharaoh, and on all his house, before our eyes;"

PRAYER:

Father, in the name of Jesus Christ, I ask that You show great and awesome signs and wonders on my life and on all my household, before everyone.

DAILY REFLECTION:

Take a moment to reflect on the Bible verse(s) for today and write your thoughts below:

August 26

BIBLE VERSE(S):

Jeremiah 20:11 WEB

"But Yahweh is with me as an awesome mighty one. Therefore my persecutors will stumble, and they won't prevail. They will be utterly disappointed, because they have not dealt wisely, even with an everlasting dishonor which will never be forgotten."

PRAYER:

Father, in the name of Jesus Christ, I decree and declare that You, Yahweh, are with me as an awesome mighty one. Therefore, my persecutors will stumble, and they won't prevail. They will be utterly disappointed.

DAILY REFLECTION:

Take a moment to reflect on the Bible verse(s) for today and write your thoughts below:

August 27

BIBLE VERSE(S):

Joel 2:11 WEB

"Yahweh thunders his voice before his army; for his forces are very great; for he is strong who obeys his command; for the day of Yahweh is great and very awesome, and who can endure it?"

PRAYER:

Father, in the name of Jesus Christ, I decree and declare Your greatness over this day. Your day is great and very awesome.

DAILY REFLECTION:

Take a moment to reflect on the Bible verse(s) for today and write your thoughts below:

BIBLE VERSE(S):

Psalm 66:1 NKJV

"Praise to God for His Awesome Works To the Chief Musician. A Song. A Psalm. Make a joyful shout to God, all the earth!"

PRAYER:

Father, in the name of Jesus Christ, I praise You for Your awesome works. I make a joyful shout to God!

DAILY REFLECTION:

Take a moment to reflect on the Bible verse(s) for today and write your thoughts below:

August 29

BIBLE VERSE(S):

Job 25:2 NIV

"Dominion and awe belong to God; he establishes order in the heights of heaven."

PRAYER:

Father, in the name of Jesus Christ, I decree and declare that dominion and awesome might belong to God. As He establishes peace and order in the heights of heaven, so shall He establish peace and order in my life.

DAILY REFLECTION:

Take a moment to reflect on the Bible verse(s) for today and write your thoughts below:

August 30

BIBLE VERSE(S):

Psalm 17:7 NLT

"Show me your unfailing love in wonderful ways. By your mighty power you rescue those who seek refuge from their enemies."

PRAYER:

Father, in the name of Jesus Christ, I decree and declare that You shall show me Your unfailing love in wonderful ways. By Your mighty power You shall rescue me from my enemies.

DAILY REFLECTION:

Take a moment to reflect on the Bible verse(s) for today and write your thoughts below:

August 31

BIBLE VERSE(S):

Psalm 46:8 MSG

"Attention, all! See the marvels of God!"

PRAYER:

Father, in the name of Jesus Christ, I decree and declare that I shall pay attention to see Your marvels. I acknowledge and thank You for all the marvelous things You have done in and around my life.

DAILY REFLECTION:

Take a moment to reflect on the Bible verse(s) for today and write your thoughts below:

Thank You Lord for the superb signs and the powerful miracles that You have worked and will continue to work in our lives in Jesus name.

CHAPTER 9

Superb September

I'm delighted to share the signs and miracles that the Most High God has worked in my life. His signs are superb! His miracles so powerful! His kingdom is everlasting. His rule is for all time.
Daniel 4:2-3 CEB

Welcome to Superb September!

In this month, you will reflect on the superb power of God.

I love this month's prayer theme because the Scriptures showcase the supernatural power of God and serve as a reminder of God's supremacy in the affairs of humanity.

As you pray and make declarations about the superb power of God, you will see God perform superb signs and wonders in and through your life in the mighty name of Jesus Christ.

September 1

BIBLE VERSE(S):

Daniel 4:3 NASB

"How great are His signs And how mighty are His miracles! His kingdom is an everlasting kingdom, And His dominion is from generation to generation."

PRAYER:

Father, in the name of Jesus Christ, I ask that You perform superb signs and powerful miracles in my life today and in the month of September.

DAILY REFLECTION:

Take a moment to reflect on the Bible verse(s) for today and write your thoughts below:

September 2

BIBLE VERSE(S):

Exodus 8:19 AMP

"Then the magicians said to Pharaoh, 'This is the [supernatural] finger of God.' But Pharaoh's heart was hardened and he would not listen to them, just as the Lord had said."

PRAYER:

Father, in the name of Jesus Christ, I ask that You place Your supernatural finger upon my life and family.

DAILY REFLECTION:

Take a moment to reflect on the Bible verse(s) for today and write your thoughts below:

BIBLE VERSE(S):

Exodus 10:23 AMP

"The Egyptians could not see one another, nor did anyone leave his place for three days, but all the Israelites had [supernatural] light in their dwellings."

PRAYER:

Father, in the name of Jesus Christ, I ask that when darkness increases in the world, let Your supernatural light shine brighter and brighter.

DAILY REFLECTION:

Take a moment to reflect on the Bible verse(s) for today and write your thoughts below:

September 4

BIBLE VERSE(S):

1 Kings 18:46 AMP

"Then the hand of the Lord came upon Elijah [giving him supernatural strength]. He girded up his loins and outran Ahab to the entrance of Jezreel [nearly twenty miles]."

PRAYER:

Father, in the name of Jesus Christ, I ask that You place Your hand upon me and give me supernatural strength to fulfil my destiny for Your glory.

DAILY REFLECTION:

Take a moment to reflect on the Bible verse(s) for today and write your thoughts below:

September 5

BIBLE VERSE(S):

John 1:12-13 AMP

"But to as many as did receive and welcome Him, He gave the right [the authority, the privilege] to become children of God, that is, to those who believe in (adhere to, trust in, and rely on) His name—who were born, not of blood [natural conception], nor of the will of the flesh [physical impulse], nor of the will of man [that of a natural father], but of God [that is, a divine and supernatural birth—they are born of God—spiritually transformed, renewed, sanctified]."

PRAYER:

Father, in the name of Jesus Christ, I thank You for giving me the right, authority and privilege to be Your child. I decree and declare that I believe in the name of Jesus, I am born of God through a divine and supernatural birth—spiritually transformed, renewed and sanctified.

DAILY REFLECTION:

Take a moment to reflect on the Bible verse(s) for today and write your thoughts below:

September 6

BIBLE VERSE(S):

John 1:16 AMP

"For out of His fullness [the superabundance of His grace and truth] we have all received grace upon grace [spiritual blessing upon spiritual blessing, favor upon favor, and gift heaped upon gift]."

PRAYER:

Father, in the name of Jesus Christ, I thank You that out of Your I have all received grace upon grace.

DAILY REFLECTION:

Take a moment to reflect on the Bible verse(s) for today and write your thoughts below:

September 7

BIBLE VERSE(S):

Genesis 35:5 AMP

"As they journeyed, there was a great [supernatural] terror [sent from God] on the cities around them, and [for that reason] the Canaanites did not pursue the sons of Jacob."

PRAYER:

Father, in the name of Jesus Christ, let Your supernatural power and superb wonders be evident in my life and all that concerns me.

DAILY REFLECTION:

Take a moment to reflect on the Bible verse(s) for today and write your thoughts below:

September 8

BIBLE VERSE(S):

Galatians 4:31 AMP

"So then, believers, we [who are born again—reborn from above—spiritually transformed, renewed, and set apart for His purpose] are not children of a slave woman [the natural], but of the free woman [the supernatural]."

PRAYER:

Father, in the name of Jesus Christ, I thank You that I am born again—reborn from above. I decree and declare that I am spiritually transformed, renewed, and set apart for Your purpose.

DAILY REFLECTION:

Take a moment to reflect on the Bible verse(s) for today and write your thoughts below:

BIBLE VERSE(S):

Ephesians 3:20 AMP

"Now to Him who is able to [carry out His purpose and] do superabundantly more than all that we dare ask or think [infinitely beyond our greatest prayers, hopes, or dreams], according to His power that is at work within us,"

PRAYER:

Father, in the name of Jesus Christ, I ask that You do superabundantly more than all that I ask or think, according to Your power that is at work within me.

DAILY REFLECTION:

Take a moment to reflect on the Bible verse(s) for today and write your thoughts below:

September 10

BIBLE VERSE(S):

Ephesians 6:12-13 AMP

"For our struggle is not against flesh and blood [contending only with physical opponents], but against the rulers, against the powers, against the world forces of this [present] darkness, against the spiritual forces of wickedness in the heavenly (supernatural) places. Therefore, put on the complete armor of God, so that you will be able to [successfully] resist and stand your ground in the evil day [of danger], and having done everything [that the crisis demands], to stand firm [in your place, fully prepared, immovable, victorious]."

PRAYER:

Father, in the name of Jesus Christ, I thank You for the revelation that our struggle is not against flesh and blood. Please help me to keep on the complete armor of God, so that I will be able to resist and stand my ground in the evil day, and having done everything, to stand firm.

DAILY REFLECTION:

Take a moment to reflect on the Bible verse(s) for today and write your thoughts below:

____

____

____

September 11

BIBLE VERSE(S):

Philippians 1:19 AMP

"for I know [with confidence] that this will turn out for my deliverance and spiritual well-being, through your prayers and the [superabundant] supply of the Spirit of Jesus Christ [which upholds me]."

PRAYER:

Father, in the name of Jesus Christ, I ask that You bless me with a "superabundant" supply of the Spirit of Jesus Christ to uphold me today and always.

DAILY REFLECTION:

Take a moment to reflect on the Bible verse(s) for today and write your thoughts below:

September 12

BIBLE VERSE(S):

1 Timothy 1:14 AMP

"The grace of our Lord [His amazing, unmerited favor and blessing] flowed out in superabundance [for me, together] with the faith and love which are [realized] in Christ Jesus."

PRAYER:

Father, in the name of Jesus Christ, I decree and declare that the grace of our Lord shall continue to flow out in superabundance with the faith and love which are realized in Christ Jesus.

DAILY REFLECTION:

Take a moment to reflect on the Bible verse(s) for today and write your thoughts below:

September 13

BIBLE VERSE(S):

1 Thessalonians 2:13 AMP

"And we also thank God continually for this, that when you received the word of God [concerning salvation] which you heard from us, you welcomed it not as the word of [mere] men, but as it truly is, the word of God, which is effectually at work in you who believe [exercising its inherent, supernatural power in those of faith]."

PRAYER:

Father, in the name of Jesus Christ, I thank You continually for the word of God, which is effectually at work in me—exercising its inherent, supernatural power.

DAILY REFLECTION:

Take a moment to reflect on the Bible verse(s) for today and write your thoughts below:

September 14

BIBLE VERSE(S):

Colossians 2:15 AMP

"When He had disarmed the rulers and authorities [those supernatural forces of evil operating against us], He made a public example of them [exhibiting them as captives in His triumphal procession], having triumphed over them through the cross."

PRAYER:

Lord Jesus Christ, I thank You for a life of victory, for You have disarmed the rulers and authorities and made a public example of them having triumphed over them through the cross.

DAILY REFLECTION:

Take a moment to reflect on the Bible verse(s) for today and write your thoughts below:

BIBLE VERSE(S):

Daniel 5:14 NKJV

"I have heard of you, that the Spirit of God is in you, and that light and understanding and excellent wisdom are found in you."

PRAYER:

Father, in the name of Jesus Christ, I decree and declare that because I have the Spirit of God in me, light and understanding and superior and excellent wisdom are found in me.

DAILY REFLECTION:

Take a moment to reflect on the Bible verse(s) for today and write your thoughts below:

September 16

BIBLE VERSE(S):

Romans 5:20 AMP

"But the Law came to increase and expand [the awareness of] the trespass [by defining and unmasking sin]. But where sin increased, [God's remarkable, gracious gift of] grace [His unmerited favor] has surpassed it and increased all the more..."

PRAYER:

Father, in the name of Jesus Christ, I decree and declare that Your grace increases the more and superabounds in my life and all that concerns me.

DAILY REFLECTION:

Take a moment to reflect on the Bible verse(s) for today and write your thoughts below:

BIBLE VERSE(S):

1 Corinthians 10:3-4 NKJV

"...all ate the same spiritual food, and all drank the same spiritual drink. For they drank of that spiritual Rock that followed them, and that Rock was Christ."

PRAYER:

Father, in the name of Jesus Christ, I ask that You let me eat and drink the spiritual—supernaturally given—food and drink from the Rock, which is Christ Jesus, all the days of my life.

DAILY REFLECTION:

Take a moment to reflect on the Bible verse(s) for today and write your thoughts below:

September 18

BIBLE VERSE(S):

Isaiah 28:29 NKJV

"This also comes from the Lord of hosts, Who is wonderful in counsel and excellent in guidance."

PRAYER:

Father, in the name of Jesus Christ, I ask that You give me supernatural and excellent guidance and impart Your wonderful wisdom and counsel upon me.

Daily Reflection:

Take a moment to reflect on the Bible verse(s) for today and write your thoughts below:

BIBLE VERSE(S):

Colossians 1:29 AMP

"For this I labor [often to the point of exhaustion], striving with His power and energy, which so greatly works within me."

PRAYER:

Father, in the name of Jesus Christ, I ask that You mightily enkindle and work within me Your great power and energy.

DAILY REFLECTION:

Take a moment to reflect on the Bible verse(s) for today and write your thoughts below:

BIBLE VERSE(S):

Psalm 95:3 NLT

"For the Lord is a great God, a great King above all gods."

PRAYER:

Father, in the name of Jesus Christ, I decree and declare that You are a great God, a great King who is above and superior to all gods.

DAILY REFLECTION:

Take a moment to reflect on the Bible verse(s) for today and write your thoughts below:

September 21

BIBLE VERSE(S):

Psalm 135:5 NLT

"Yes, I know the Lord is great, and our Lord is superior to all gods."

PRAYER:

Father, in the name of Jesus Christ, I decree and declare again that I know that You are great. You are superior to all gods.

DAILY REFLECTION:

Take a moment to reflect on the Bible verse(s) for today and write your thoughts below:

September 22

BIBLE VERSE(S):

Daniel 4:2 NLT

"I want you all to know about the miraculous signs and wonders the Most High God has performed for me."

PRAYER:

Father, in the name of Jesus Christ, I decree and declare that I will continuously share the miraculous signs and wonders that You have performed for me for Your glory.

DAILY REFLECTION:

Take a moment to reflect on the Bible verse(s) for today and write your thoughts below:

September 23

BIBLE VERSE(S):

Daniel 4:3 CEB

"His signs are superb! His miracles so powerful! His kingdom is everlasting. His rule is for all time."

PRAYER:

Father, in the name of Jesus Christ, I thank You that Your signs in my life are superb and Your miracles in my life are so powerful.

DAILY REFLECTION:

Take a moment to reflect on the Bible verse(s) for today and write your thoughts below:

September 24

BIBLE VERSE(S):

Hebrews 1:3-4 NLT

"The Son radiates God's own glory and expresses the very character of God, and he sustains everything by the mighty power of his command. When he had cleansed us from our sins, he sat down in the place of honor at the right hand of the majestic God in heaven. This shows that the Son is far greater than the angels, just as the name God gave him is greater than their names."

PRAYER:

Father, in the name of Jesus Christ, I thank You for the gift of Your Son, Jesus Christ, Who is the radiance of Your glory and the exact expression of Your nature, sustaining all things by Your powerful Word.

DAILY REFLECTION:

Take a moment to reflect on the Bible verse(s) for today and write your thoughts below:

BIBLE VERSE(S):

Psalm 66:12 TLB

"You sent troops to ride across our broken bodies. We went through fire and flood. But in the end, you brought us into wealth and great abundance."

PRAYER:

Father, in the name of Jesus Christ, I ask that You bring me into wealth and great abundance.

DAILY REFLECTION:

Take a moment to reflect on the Bible verse(s) for today and write your thoughts below:

September 26

BIBLE VERSE(S):

Exodus 7:3 AMP

"And I will make Pharaoh's heart hard, and multiply My signs and My wonders (miracles) in the land of Egypt."

PRAYER:

Father, in the name of Jesus Christ, I ask that You multiply Your signs, Your wonders, and miracles in my life and family.

DAILY REFLECTION:

Take a moment to reflect on the Bible verse(s) for today and write your thoughts below:

BIBLE VERSE(S):

Exodus 10:1 AMP

"Now the Lord said to Moses, 'Go in to Pharaoh; for I have hardened his heart and the hearts of his servants, that I may show these signs of Mine before him...'"

PRAYER:

Father, in the name of Jesus Christ, I ask that You show Your signs of divine power before my enemies as You give me victory over them.

DAILY REFLECTION:

Take a moment to reflect on the Bible verse(s) for today and write your thoughts below:

September 28

BIBLE VERSE(S):

Exodus 10:2 AMP

"And that you may recount in the ears of your son and of your grandson what I have done in derision of the Egyptians and what things I have [repeatedly] done there—My signs [of divine power] done among them—that you may recognize and know that I am the Lord."

PRAYER:

Father, in the name of Jesus Christ, I receive the grace to recount in the ears of my children and grandchildren and others what You have done for me—Your signs of divine power—that they may recognize and know that You are Lord.

DAILY REFLECTION:

Take a moment to reflect on the Bible verse(s) for today and write your thoughts below:

September 29

BIBLE VERSE(S):

Deuteronomy 7:19 AMP

"...the great trials which you saw with your own eyes, and the signs, the wonders, the mighty hand and the outstretched arm by which the Lord your God brought you out. So shall the Lord your God do to all the peoples of whom you are afraid."

PRAYER:

Father, in the name of Jesus Christ, I thank You for deliverance from all the people of whom I am afraid, through Your signs, Your wonders, and Your mighty hand and outstretched arm.

DAILY REFLECTION:

Take a moment to reflect on the Bible verse(s) for today and write your thoughts below:

BIBLE VERSE(S):

Deuteronomy 26:8 AMP

"...and the Lord brought us out of Egypt with a mighty hand and with an outstretched arm and with great terror [suffered by the Egyptians] and with signs and with wonders;"

PRAYER:

Father, in the name of Jesus Christ, I thank You for bringing me out of every form of bondage with Your mighty hand and outstretched arm, with great power, and with signs and wonders.

DAILY REFLECTION:

Take a moment to reflect on the Bible verse(s) for today and write your thoughts below:

Father, let there be an overflow of Your blessings and favor in our lives in the month of October and beyond, in Jesus name.

CHAPTER 10

October Overflow

You prepare a feast for me in the presence of my enemies. You honor me by anointing my head with oil. My cup overflows with blessings.
Psalms 23:5 NLT

Welcome to October Overflow!

The Almighty God has the ability to go above and beyond your expectations to bless you. He is a God of limitless blessings. How wonderful it is to be connected to a God Who is an infinite source of blessings.

In this month of October, as you pray and decree the promises and blessings of God over your life, you will enjoy an overflow of God's grace and blessings.

For it is written in Ephesians 3:20-21 (NKJV), "God is able to do exceedingly abundantly, above all that we can ask or think".

BIBLE VERSE(S):

Proverbs 3:10 NKJV

"So your barns will be filled with plenty, And your vats will overflow with new wine."

PRAYER:

Father, in the name of Jesus Christ, I decree and declare that my storage places—my finances, my business, the works of my hands—shall be filled with plenty and my vats shall be overflowing with new wine in this month of October and beyond.

DAILY REFLECTION:

Take a moment to reflect on the Bible verse(s) for today and write your thoughts below:

BIBLE VERSE(S):

Isaiah 66:12 ESV

"For thus says the Lord: Behold, I will extend peace to her like a river, and the glory of the nations like an overflowing stream; and you shall nurse, you shall be carried upon her hip, and bounced upon her knees."

PRAYER:

Father, in the name of Jesus Christ, I decree and declare that You extend peace to me like a river, and the glory of the nations like an overflowing stream.

DAILY REFLECTION:

Take a moment to reflect on the Bible verse(s) for today and write your thoughts below:

October 3

BIBLE VERSE(S):

Amos 9:13 AMP

"Behold, the days are coming, says the Lord, that the plowman shall overtake the reaper, and the treader of grapes him who sows the seed; and the mountains shall drop sweet wine and all the hills shall melt [that is, everything heretofore barren and unfruitful shall overflow with spiritual blessing]."

PRAYER:

Father, in the name of Jesus Christ, I ask that You bless me with an overflow of spiritual blessings.

DAILY REFLECTION:

Take a moment to reflect on the Bible verse(s) for today and write your thoughts below:

October 4

BIBLE VERSE(S):

Zechariah 1:17 AMP

"Proclaim again, 'Thus says the Lord of hosts, "My cities shall again overflow with prosperity, and the Lord shall again comfort Zion and again choose Jerusalem."'"

PRAYER:

Father, in the name of Jesus Christ, I ask that You bless me with an overflow of prosperity.

DAILY REFLECTION:

Take a moment to reflect on the Bible verse(s) for today and write your thoughts below:

October 5

BIBLE VERSE(S):

John 10:10 AMP

"The thief comes only in order to steal and kill and destroy. I came that they may have and enjoy life, and have it in abundance [to the full, till it overflows]."

PRAYER:

Father, in the name of Jesus Christ, I decree and declare that I shall continue to enjoy the life of abundance You came to give me to the full, till it overflows.

DAILY REFLECTION:

Take a moment to reflect on the Bible verse(s) for today and write your thoughts below:

BIBLE VERSE(S):

John 15:11 AMP

"I have told you these things so that My joy and delight may be in you, and that your joy may be made full and complete and overflowing."

PRAYER:

Father, in the name of Jesus Christ, I decree and declare that Your joy and delight are in me, and my joy and gladness are of full measure, complete, and overflowing.

DAILY REFLECTION:

Take a moment to reflect on the Bible verse(s) for today and write your thoughts below:

October 7

BIBLE VERSE(S):

Romans 5:15 AMP

"But the free gift [of God] is not like the trespass [because the gift of grace overwhelms the fall of man]. For if many died by one man's trespass [Adam's sin], much more [abundantly] did God's grace and the gift [that comes] by the grace of the one Man, Jesus Christ, overflow to [benefit] the many."

PRAYER:

Father, in the name of Jesus Christ, I ask that Your grace and favor abound and overflow in my life and all that concerns me.

DAILY REFLECTION:

Take a moment to reflect on the Bible verse(s) for today and write your thoughts below:

October 8

BIBLE VERSE(S):

Romans 5:17 AMP

"For if by the trespass of the one (Adam), death reigned through the one (Adam), much more surely will those who receive the abundance of grace and the free gift of righteousness reign in [eternal] life through the One, Jesus Christ."

PRAYER:

Father, in the name of Jesus Christ, I decree and declare that as I receive Your overflowing abundant grace and the free gift of righteousness, that I will reign as a king in life through Jesus Christ.

DAILY REFLECTION:

Take a moment to reflect on the Bible verse(s) for today and write your thoughts below:

BIBLE VERSE(S):

Romans 15:13 AMP

"May the God of hope fill you with all joy and peace in believing [through the experience of your faith] that by the power of the Holy Spirit you will abound in hope and overflow with confidence in His promises."

PRAYER:

Father, in the name of Jesus Christ, I ask that You fill me with all joy and peace in believing—through the experience of my faith—that by the power of the Holy Spirit I may abound and be overflowing with hope.

DAILY REFLECTION:

Take a moment to reflect on the Bible verse(s) for today and write your thoughts below:

BIBLE VERSE(S):

2 Corinthians 7:4 AMP

"Great is my confidence in you; great is my pride and boasting on your behalf. I am filled [to the brim] with comfort; I am overflowing with joy in spite of all our trouble."

PRAYER:

Father, in the name of Jesus Christ, I decree and declare that I am overflowing with joy.

DAILY REFLECTION:

Take a moment to reflect on the Bible verse(s) for today and write your thoughts below:

October 11

BIBLE VERSE(S):

Colossians 2:7 AMP

"...having been deeply rooted [in Him] and now being continually built up in Him and [becoming increasingly more] established [a]in your faith, just as you were taught, and overflowing in it with gratitude."

PRAYER:

Father, in the name of Jesus Christ, I decree and declare that I am abounding and overflowing with thanksgiving, for I am firmly and deeply planted in You and continually built up in You.

DAILY REFLECTION:

Take a moment to reflect on the Bible verse(s) for today and write your thoughts below:

October 12

BIBLE VERSE(S):

1 Thessalonians 3:12 AMP

"And may the Lord cause you to increase and excel and overflow in love for one another, and for all people, just as we also do for you;"

PRAYER:

Father, in the name of Jesus Christ, I ask that You cause me to increase and excel and overflow in love for all people.

DAILY REFLECTION:

Take a moment to reflect on the Bible verse(s) for today and write your thoughts below:

October 13

BIBLE VERSE(S):

Psalm 23:5 NIV

"You prepare a table before me in the presence of my enemies. You anoint my head with oil; my cup overflows."

PRAYER:

Father, in the name of Jesus Christ, I ask that You prepare a table before me in the presence of my enemies, anoint my head with oil and let my cup overflow.

DAILY REFLECTION:

Take a moment to reflect on the Bible verse(s) for today and write your thoughts below:

BIBLE VERSE(S):

Psalm 65:11 NIV

"You crown the year with your bounty, and your carts overflow with abundance."

PRAYER:

Father, in the name of Jesus Christ, I ask that You bless me with an overflow of abundance.

DAILY REFLECTION:

Take a moment to reflect on the Bible verse(s) for today and write your thoughts below:

BIBLE VERSE(S):

Psalm 119:171 NIV

"May my lips overflow with praise, for you teach me your decrees."

PRAYER:

Father, in the name of Jesus Christ, I decree and declare that my lips shall overflow with praise, for You teach me your decrees.

DAILY REFLECTION:

Take a moment to reflect on the Bible verse(s) for today and write your thoughts below:

October 16

BIBLE VERSE(S):

Proverbs 3:10 NIV

"...then your barns will be filled to overflowing, and your vats will brim over with new wine."

PRAYER:

Father, in the name of Jesus Christ, I ask that You let my barns be filled to overflowing and my vats brim over with new wine.

DAILY REFLECTION:

Take a moment to reflect on the Bible verse(s) for today and write your thoughts below:

BIBLE VERSE(S):

Romans 15:13 NIV

"May the God of hope fill you with all joy and peace as you trust in him, so that you may overflow with hope by the power of the Holy Spirit."

PRAYER:

Father in the name of Jesus Christ, I decree and declare that You fill me with all joy and peace and I overflow with hope by the power of the Holy Spirit as I trust in You.

DAILY REFLECTION:

Take a moment to reflect on the Bible verse(s) for today and write your thoughts below:

October 18

BIBLE VERSE(S):

2 Corinthians 4:15 NIV

"All this is for your benefit, so that the grace that is reaching more and more people may cause thanksgiving to overflow to the glory of God."

PRAYER:

Father in the name of Jesus Christ, I decree and declare that Your grace reaches more and more people causing thanksgiving to overflow to Your glory.

DAILY REFLECTION:

Take a moment to reflect on the Bible verse(s) for today and write your thoughts below:

October 19

BIBLE VERSE(S):

2 Corinthians 9:12 AMP

"For the ministry of this service (offering) is not only supplying the needs of the saints (God's people), but is also overflowing through many expressions of thanksgiving to God."

PRAYER:

Father, in the name of Jesus Christ, I thank You for an overflow in many expressions of supplying the needs of Your people in my service to You.

DAILY REFLECTION:

Take a moment to reflect on the Bible verse(s) for today and write your thoughts below:

BIBLE VERSE(S):

Psalm 65:11 AMP

"You crown the year with Your bounty, And Your paths overflow."

PRAYER:

Father, in the name of Jesus Christ, I decree and declare that You crown my years with Your goodness and my paths overflow with rich food.

DAILY REFLECTION:

Take a moment to reflect on the Bible verse(s) for today and write your thoughts below:

BIBLE VERSE(S):

Isaiah 66:12 AMP

"For the Lord says this, 'Behold, I extend peace to her (Jerusalem) like a river, And the glory of the nations like an overflowing stream; And you will be nursed, you will be carried on her hip and [playfully] rocked on her knees.'"

PRAYER:

Father, in the name of Jesus Christ, I decree and declare that You shall extend peace and prosperity to me like a river, and the wealth of nations like an overflowing stream.

DAILY REFLECTION:

Take a moment to reflect on the Bible verse(s) for today and write your thoughts below:

BIBLE VERSE(S):

Luke 6:38 NKJV

"Give, and it will be given to you: good measure, pressed down, shaken together, and running over will be put into your bosom. For with the same measure that you use, it will be measured back to you."

PRAYER:

Father, in the name of Jesus Christ, I thank You for Your promise of an overflow of a good measure, pressed down, shaken together, and running over when I give. Help me to be more generous in my giving.

DAILY REFLECTION:

Take a moment to reflect on the Bible verse(s) for today and write your thoughts below:

October 23

BIBLE VERSE(S):

Luke 10:21 AMP

"In that very hour He was overjoyed and rejoiced greatly in the Holy Spirit, and He said, "I praise You, O Father, Lord of heaven and earth, that You have hidden these things [relating to salvation] from the wise and intelligent, and have revealed them to infants [the childlike and untaught]."

PRAYER:

Father, in the name of Jesus Christ, let me overflow with joy from the Holy Spirit as You show me things You've hidden from the wise and intelligent.

DAILY REFLECTION:

Take a moment to reflect on the Bible verse(s) for today and write your thoughts below:

BIBLE VERSE(S):

Acts 13:52 NLT

"And the believers were filled with joy and with the Holy Spirit."

PRAYER:

Father, in the name of Jesus Christ, I decree and declare that I overflow with joy because of the abundant presence of the Holy Spirit.

DAILY REFLECTION:

Take a moment to reflect on the Bible verse(s) for today and write your thoughts below:

October 25

BIBLE VERSE(S):

Romans 15:13 NIV

"May the God of hope fill you with all joy and peace as you trust in him, so that you may overflow with hope by the power of the Holy Spirit."

PRAYER:

Father, in the name of Jesus Christ, I ask that You fill me with all joy and peace in faith so that I overflow with hope by the power of the Holy Spirit.

DAILY REFLECTION:

Take a moment to reflect on the Bible verse(s) for today and write your thoughts below:

October 26

BIBLE VERSE(S):

Ephesians 1:7 NIV

"In him we have redemption through his blood, the forgiveness of sins, in accordance with the riches of God's grace."

PRAYER:

Father, in the name of Jesus Christ, I thank You because I have been redeemed through the blood of Jesus Christ, and I have forgiveness for my failures based on His overflowing grace.

DAILY REFLECTION:

Take a moment to reflect on the Bible verse(s) for today and write your thoughts below:

BIBLE VERSE(S):

James 3:17-18 MSG

"Real wisdom, God's wisdom, begins with a holy life and is characterized by getting along with others. It is gentle and reasonable, overflowing with mercy and blessings, not hot one day and cold the next, not two-faced. You can develop a healthy, robust community that lives right with God and enjoy its results only if you do the hard work of getting along with each other, treating each other with dignity and honor."

PRAYER:

Father, in the name of Jesus Christ, I ask for real wisdom, Your wisdom, that begins with a holy life and is characterized by getting along with others, is gentle and reasonable, and overflowing with mercy and blessings.

DAILY REFLECTION:

Take a moment to reflect on the Bible verse(s) for today and write your thoughts below:

BIBLE VERSE(S):

1 Timothy 1:14 ESV

"...and the grace of our Lord overflowed for me with the faith and love that are in Christ Jesus."

PRAYER:

Father, in the name of Jesus Christ, I decree and declare that the grace of our Lord overflows for me with the faith and love that are in Christ Jesus.

DAILY REFLECTION:

Take a moment to reflect on the Bible verse(s) for today and write your thoughts below:

October 29

BIBLE VERSE(S):

John 16:21-24 MSG

"When a woman gives birth, she has a hard time, there's no getting around it. But when the baby is born, there is joy in the birth. This new life in the world wipes out memory of the pain. The sadness you have right now is similar to that pain, but the coming joy is also similar. When I see you again, you'll be full of joy, and it will be a joy no one can rob from you. You'll no longer be so full of questions. 'This is what I want you to do: Ask the Father for whatever is in keeping with the things I've revealed to you. Ask in my name, according to my will, and he'll most certainly give it to you. Your joy will be a river overflowing its banks!'"

PRAYER:

Father, in the name of Jesus Christ, I thank You because You'll most certainly give me what I ask for in the name of Jesus and according to Your will, and my joy will be a river overflowing its banks.

DAILY REFLECTION:

Take a moment to reflect on the Bible verse(s) for today and write your thoughts below:

___

___

___

BIBLE VERSE(S):

Deuteronomy 33:23 AMP

"Of Naphtali he said, 'O Naphtali, satisfied with favor, And full of the blessing of the Lord, Take possession of the sea [of Galilee] and the south.'"

PRAYER:

Father, in the name of Jesus Christ, I decree and declare that I am overflowing with favor, and I am full of the Lord's blessing.

DAILY REFLECTION:

Take a moment to reflect on the Bible verse(s) for today and write your thoughts below:

BIBLE VERSE(S):

2 Corinthians 9:8 NLT

"And God will generously provide all you need. Then you will always have everything you need and plenty left over to share with others."

PRAYER:

Father, in the name of Jesus Christ, I decree and declare that You will generously provide all I need. Then I will always have everything I need, and plenty left over and overflowing to share with others.

DAILY REFLECTION:

Take a moment to reflect on the Bible verse(s) for today and write your thoughts below:

Thank You Father for taking us to new levels of blessings in November and beyond, in Jesus name.

CHAPTER 11

New Level November

Behold, I am doing a new thing; now it springs forth, do you not perceive it? I will make a way in the wilderness and rivers in the desert.
Isaiah 43:19 ESV

Welcome to New Level November!

I don't consider myself to be a morning person. In fact, as soon as I hear my alarm go off in the morning, I hit the snooze button just to get at least 5 minutes of extra deep sleep, so I tend to set my alarm about 10 minutes prior to my anticipated "wake up" time (as my older son calls it) to ensure that I enjoy what is left of my sweet early morning sleep.

However, mornings have become a constant reminder of the fresh start accorded to us by Jesus Christ. We are a new creation; old things have passed away[5]*. They are over and done with—forever!*

The novelty of every morning reminds me of the new blessings, new favor, new opportunities, new dreams, new goals, new mercies, new ideas, new joy, new anointing, new grace, new peace, new miracles, and new testimonies that Jesus Christ has in store for us. All brand new!

I pray that as you wake up to a new morning, you will have a newfound appreciation for your new life and that the novelty of each morning will never ever wear off in the precious name of Jesus Christ.

---

5 "Therefore, if anyone is in Christ, he is a new creation; old things have passed away; behold, all things have become new" (2 Corinthians 5:17, NKJV).

November 1

BIBLE VERSE(S):

Psalm 40:3 NLT

"He has given me a new song to sing, a hymn of praise to our God. Many will see what he has done and be amazed. They will put their trust in the Lord."

PRAYER:

Father, in the name of Jesus Christ, I thank You for giving me reason to sing a new song, a hymn of praise to You in this new month of November and beyond. May many see what You have done in my life and be amazed and put their trust in You, Lord.

DAILY REFLECTION:

Take a moment to reflect on the Bible verse(s) for today and write your thoughts below:

BIBLE VERSE(S):

Genesis 27:28 NLT

"From the dew of heaven and the richness of the earth, may God always give you abundant harvests of grain and bountiful new wine."

PRAYER:

Father, in the name of Jesus Christ, I ask that You give me the dew of heaven and the richness of the earth, and abundant harvests of grain and bountiful new wine.

DAILY REFLECTION:

Take a moment to reflect on the Bible verse(s) for today and write your thoughts below:

November 3

BIBLE VERSE(S):

Leviticus 26:10 NIV

"You will still be eating last year's harvest when you will have to move it out to make room for the new."

PRAYER:

Father, in the name of Jesus Christ, as I approach the end of the year, I make room for new blessings from You.

DAILY REFLECTION:

Take a moment to reflect on the Bible verse(s) for today and write your thoughts below:

BIBLE VERSE(S):

Deuteronomy 7:13 AMP

"He will love you and bless you and multiply you; He will also bless the fruit of your womb and the fruit of your land, your grain and your new wine and your [olive] oil, the offspring of your cattle and the young of your flock, in the land which He swore to your fathers to give you."

PRAYER:

Father, in the name of Jesus Christ, I decree and declare that You will love and bless me and multiply me. Thank You, Lord, that You will bless me and my children in the land which You swore to my fathers to give me.

DAILY REFLECTION:

Take a moment to reflect on the Bible verse(s) for today and write your thoughts below:

November 5

BIBLE VERSE(S):

Deuteronomy 11:14 NLT

"...then he will send the rains in their proper seasons—the early and late rains—so you can bring in your harvests of grain, new wine, and olive oil."

PRAYER:

Father, in the name of Jesus Christ, I decree and declare Your promise over my life – that You will send rains in their proper seasons so I can bring in harvests of new blessings.

DAILY REFLECTION:

Take a moment to reflect on the Bible verse(s) for today and write your thoughts below:

BIBLE VERSE(S):

Psalm 33:3 NIV

"Sing to him a new song; play skillfully, and shout for joy."

PRAYER:

Father, in the name of Jesus Christ, I sing a new song to You. I shout out praises to You today, for You alone are worthy.

DAILY REFLECTION:

Take a moment to reflect on the Bible verse(s) for today and write your thoughts below:

November 7

BIBLE VERSE(S):

2 Corinthians 5:17 NLT

"This means that anyone who belongs to Christ has become a new person. The old life is gone; a new life has begun!"

PRAYER:

Father, in the name of Jesus Christ, I decree and declare that I belong to Jesus Christ, and I have become a new person. The old life is gone, and a new life has begun.

DAILY REFLECTION:

Take a moment to reflect on the Bible verse(s) for today and write your thoughts below:

November 8

BIBLE VERSE(S):

Psalm 96:1 NLT

Sing a new song to the Lord! Let the whole earth sing to the Lord!"

PRAYER:

Father, in the name of Jesus Christ, I thank You for giving me a new song to sing to You. I sing praises to You, Lord, now and forever. Hallelujah!

DAILY REFLECTION:

Take a moment to reflect on the Bible verse(s) for today and write your thoughts below:

BIBLE VERSE(S):

Psalm 98:1 NLT

"Sing a new song to the Lord, for he has done wonderful deeds. His right hand has won a mighty victory; his holy arm has shown his saving power!"

PRAYER:

Father, in the name of Jesus Christ, I sing to You a new song, for You perform amazing deeds. Your right hand and Your mighty arm accomplish deliverance.

DAILY REFLECTION:

Take a moment to reflect on the Bible verse(s) for today and write your thoughts below:

BIBLE VERSE(S):

Psalm 144:9 NLT

"I will sing a new song to you, O God! I will sing your praises with a ten-stringed harp."

PRAYER:

Father, in the name of Jesus Christ, today I sing a new song to You. Accompanied by a ten-stringed instrument, I clap my hands as I sing praises to You.

DAILY REFLECTION:

Take a moment to reflect on the Bible verse(s) for today and write your thoughts below:

November 11

BIBLE VERSE(S):

Psalm 149:1 NLT

"Praise the Lord! Sing to the Lord a new song. Sing his praises in the assembly of the faithful."

PRAYER:

Father, in the name of Jesus Christ, I praise and sing a new song to You. I praise You in the assembly of the faithful.

DAILY REFLECTION:

Take a moment to reflect on the Bible verse(s) for today and write your thoughts below:

November 12

BIBLE VERSE(S):

Isaiah 41:15 NLT

"You will be a new threshing instrument with many sharp teeth. You will tear your enemies apart, making chaff of mountains."

PRAYER:

Father, in the name of Jesus Christ, I decree and declare that You are making me a new threshing instrument with many sharp teeth. I will tear my enemies apart, making chaff of mountains.

DAILY REFLECTION:

Take a moment to reflect on the Bible verse(s) for today and write your thoughts below:

November 13

BIBLE VERSE(S):

Isaiah 43:19 NIV

"See, I am doing a new thing! Now it springs up; do you not perceive it? I am making a way in the wilderness and streams in the wasteland."

PRAYER:

Father, in the name of Jesus Christ, I receive the new things You are doing in my life. I recognize them. I decree and declare that You will make a way in the wilderness and streams in the wasteland for me.

DAILY REFLECTION:

Take a moment to reflect on the Bible verse(s) for today and write your thoughts below:

November 14

BIBLE VERSE(S):

Isaiah 62:2 NIV

"The nations will see your vindication, and all kings your glory; you will be called by a new name that the mouth of the Lord will bestow."

PRAYER:

Father, in the name of Jesus Christ, I decree and declare that nations will see my vindication, and all kings my splendor. I will be called by a new name that the Lord Himself will give me.

DAILY REFLECTION:

Take a moment to reflect on the Bible verse(s) for today and write your thoughts below:

November 15

BIBLE VERSE(S):

Isaiah 66:22 NKJV

"'For as the new heavens and the new earth Which I will make shall remain before Me,' says the Lord, 'So shall your descendants and your name remain.'"

PRAYER:

Father, in the name of Jesus Christ, I thank You for making my descendants and my name remain, just as the new heavens and the new earth You are about to make will remain standing before You.

DAILY REFLECTION:

Take a moment to reflect on the Bible verse(s) for today and write your thoughts below:

November 16

BIBLE VERSE(S):

Ezekiel 36:26 NKJV

"I will give you a new heart and put a new spirit within you; I will take the heart of stone out of your flesh and give you a heart of flesh."

PRAYER:

Father, in the name of Jesus Christ, I thank You for giving me a new heart and for putting a new spirit within me. Thank You, Lord, for removing the heart of stone from my body and giving me a heart of flesh.

DAILY REFLECTION:

Take a moment to reflect on the Bible verse(s) for today and write your thoughts below:

November 17

BIBLE VERSE(S):

Lamentations 3:22-23 NIV

"Because of the Lord's great love we are not consumed, for his compassions never fail. They are new every morning; great is your faithfulness."

PRAYER:

Father, in the name of Jesus Christ, I decree and declare that because of Your great love I am not consumed, for Your compassions never fail. They are new every morning; great is Your faithfulness.

DAILY REFLECTION:

Take a moment to reflect on the Bible verse(s) for today and write your thoughts below:

November 18

BIBLE VERSE(S):

2 Corinthians 5:17 AMP

"Therefore if anyone is in Christ [that is, grafted in, joined to Him by faith in Him as Savior], he is a new creature [reborn and renewed by the Holy Spirit]; the old things [the previous moral and spiritual condition] have passed away. Behold, new things have come [because spiritual awakening brings a new life]."

PRAYER:

Father, in the name of Jesus Christ, I thank You because I am grafted in Jesus Christ, I am a new creature, the old things—my previous moral and spiritual condition—have passed away and new things have come.

DAILY REFLECTION:

Take a moment to reflect on the Bible verse(s) for today and write your thoughts below:

November 19

BIBLE VERSE(S):

Hebrews 12:24 NIV

"...to Jesus the mediator of a new covenant, and to the sprinkled blood that speaks a better word than the blood of Abel."

PRAYER:

Father, in the name of Jesus Christ, I thank You that I have Jesus as the mediator of a new covenant, the sprinkled blood of Jesus speaks a better word in my life and all that concerns me than the blood of Abel.

DAILY REFLECTION:

Take a moment to reflect on the Bible verse(s) for today and write your thoughts below:

November 20

BIBLE VERSE(S):

1 Peter 1:3 NIV

"Praise to God for a Living Hope: Praise be to the God and Father of our Lord Jesus Christ! In his great mercy he has given us new birth into a living hope through the resurrection of Jesus Christ from the dead."

PRAYER:

Father, in the name of Jesus Christ, I praise You for a Living Hope. I praise You my God and Father of our Lord Jesus Christ. For in Your great mercy, You have given me new birth into a living hope through the resurrection of Jesus Christ from the dead.

DAILY REFLECTION:

Take a moment to reflect on the Bible verse(s) for today and write your thoughts below:

November 21

BIBLE VERSE(S):

Revelation 21:5 NIV

"He who was seated on the throne said, 'I am making everything new!' Then he said, 'Write this down, for these words are trustworthy and true.'"

PRAYER:

Father, in the name of Jesus Christ, I thank You for making everything new in my life. I believe and receive Your Words, for Your Words are trustworthy and true.

DAILY REFLECTION:

Take a moment to reflect on the Bible verse(s) for today and write your thoughts below:

November 22

BIBLE VERSE(S):

Esther 8:16 AMP

"For [at this time] the Jews had light [a dawn of new hope] and gladness and joy and honor."

PRAYER:

Father, in the name of Jesus Christ, I decree and declare that I have light, a dawn of new hope, gladness, joy, and honor.

DAILY REFLECTION:

Take a moment to reflect on the Bible verse(s) for today and write your thoughts below:

November 23

BIBLE VERSE(S):

Psalm 145:2 AMP

"Every day I will bless You and lovingly praise You; Yes, [with awe-inspired reverence] I will praise Your name forever and ever."

PRAYER:

Father, in the name of Jesus Christ, I decree and declare that I will bless You and lovingly praise You every day. I will praise Your name forever and ever.

DAILY REFLECTION:

Take a moment to reflect on the Bible verse(s) for today and write your thoughts below:

BIBLE VERSE(S):

Isaiah 48:6 AMP

"You have heard [these things foretold]; look at all this [that has been fulfilled]. And you, will you not declare it? I proclaim to you [specific] new things from this time, Even [a]hidden things which you have not known."

PRAYER:

Father, in the name of Jesus Christ, I decree and declare that You shall proclaim specific new things to me from this time forth, even hidden things which I have not known.

DAILY REFLECTION:

Take a moment to reflect on the Bible verse(s) for today and write your thoughts below:

November 25

BIBLE VERSE(S):

Isaiah 51:16 AMP

"I have put My words in your mouth and have covered you with the shadow of My hand, to establish the [renewed] heavens and lay the foundations of the [renewed] earth, and to say to Zion (Jerusalem), 'You are My people.'"

PRAYER:

Father, in the name of Jesus Christ, I thank You for putting Your words in my mouth and covering me with the shadow of Your hand, to establish the renewed heavens and lay the foundations of a renewed earth and say to me and my household, "You are My people."

DAILY REFLECTION:

Take a moment to reflect on the Bible verse(s) for today and write your thoughts below:

November 26

BIBLE VERSE(S):

Isaiah 58:8 AMP

"Then your light will break out like the dawn, And your healing (restoration, new life) will quickly spring forth; Your righteousness will go before you [leading you to peace and prosperity], The glory of the Lord will be your rear guard."

PRAYER:

Father, in the name of Jesus Christ, I decree and declare that my light shall break forth like the morning, and my healing—my restoration and the power of a new life—shall spring forth speedily; my righteousness—my rightness, my justice, and my right relationship with God—shall go before me, conducting me to peace and prosperity, and the glory of the Lord shall be my rear guard.

DAILY REFLECTION:

Take a moment to reflect on the Bible verse(s) for today and write your thoughts below:

BIBLE VERSE(S):

Isaiah 60:1 AMP

"A Glorified Zion 'Arise [from spiritual depression to a new life], shine [be radiant with the glory and brilliance of the Lord]; for your light has come, And the glory and brilliance of the Lord has risen upon you.'"

PRAYER:

Father, in the name of Jesus Christ, I decree and declare that I arise to a new life. I shine with the glory and brilliance of the Lord, for my light has come, and the glory and brilliance of the Lord has risen upon me.

DAILY REFLECTION:

Take a moment to reflect on the Bible verse(s) for today and write your thoughts below:

November 28

BIBLE VERSE(S):

Job 14:7 NLT

"Even a tree has more hope! If it is cut down, it will sprout again and grow new branches."

PRAYER:

Father, in the name of Jesus Christ, I decree and declare that just as a tree has more hope that if it is cut down, it will sprout again and grow new branches, I have hope in You for new dimensions of growth in my life.

DAILY REFLECTION:

Take a moment to reflect on the Bible verse(s) for today and write your thoughts below:

November 29

BIBLE VERSE(S):

Job 29:20 NLT

"New honors are constantly bestowed on me, and my strength is continually renewed."

PRAYER:

Father, in the name of Jesus Christ, I decree and declare that new honors are constantly bestowed on me and my strength is continually renewed.

DAILY REFLECTION:

Take a moment to reflect on the Bible verse(s) for today and write your thoughts below:

November 30

BIBLE VERSE(S):

Isaiah 40:31 NLT

"But those who trust in the Lord will find new strength. They will soar high on wings like eagles. They will run and not grow weary. They will walk and not faint."

PRAYER:

Father, in the name of Jesus Christ, I thank You because as I trust in You, I will find new strength. I will soar high on wings like eagles. I will run and not grow weary. I will walk and not faint.

DAILY REFLECTION:

Take a moment to reflect on the Bible verse(s) for today and write your thoughts below:

Thank You Heavenly Father for taking great delight in us in December and beyond.

CHAPTER 12

Delightful December

The Lord your God is with you, the Mighty Warrior who saves, He will take great delight in you; in his love he will no longer rebuke you, but will rejoice over you with singing.
Zephaniah 3:17 NIV

Welcome to Delightful December!

It is so heartwarming to know that God delights in us. I consider God's delight in us as a powerful source of validation from our Creator. Knowing that God delights in me gives me an unparalleled level of God-fidence (confidence in God), a strong sense of His love for me and the happiness He derives from me. I picture God smiling delightfully at me and my heart is filled with joy.

As you pray and make declarations that pertain to the delight of God, you will gain a greater understanding of God's delight in you. My prayer for you is that you will experience and have many testimonies of His delight in you like never before, in the mighty name of Jesus Christ.

December 1

BIBLE VERSE(S):

Deuteronomy 30:9 NIV

"Then the Lord your God will make you most prosperous in all the work of your hands and in the fruit of your womb, the young of your livestock and the crops of your land. The Lord will again delight in you and make you prosperous, just as he delighted in your ancestors,"

PRAYER:

Father, in the name of Jesus Christ, I thank You for delighting in me and making me prosperous in all the works of my hands in this new of month of December and beyond.

DAILY REFLECTION:

Take a moment to reflect on the Bible verse(s) for today and write your thoughts below:

December 2

BIBLE VERSE(S):

1 Samuel 2:1 NIV

"Hannah's Prayer: Then Hannah prayed and said: 'My heart rejoices in the Lord; in the Lord my horn is lifted high. My mouth boasts over my enemies, for I delight in your deliverance.'"

PRAYER:

Father, in the name of Jesus Christ, I decree and declare that my heart rejoices in You, Lord; in You my horn is lifted high. My mouth boasts over my enemies, for I delight in your deliverance, Lord.

DAILY REFLECTION:

Take a moment to reflect on the Bible verse(s) for today and write your thoughts below:

December 3

BIBLE VERSE(S):

2 Samuel 22:20 NIV

"He brought me out into a spacious place; he rescued me because he delighted in me."

PRAYER:

Father, in the name of Jesus Christ, I thank You for bringing me out into a spacious place. Thank You, Lord, for rescuing me because You delighted in me.

DAILY REFLECTION:

Take a moment to reflect on the Bible verse(s) for today and write your thoughts below:

BIBLE VERSE(S):

Psalm 37:4 NIV

"Take delight in the Lord, and he will give you the desires of your heart."

PRAYER:

Father, in the name of Jesus Christ, I thank You for giving me the desires of my heart as I take delight in You.

DAILY REFLECTION:

Take a moment to reflect on the Bible verse(s) for today and write your thoughts below:

December 5

BIBLE VERSE(S):

1 Kings 10:9 NIV

"Praise be to the Lord your God, who has delighted in you and placed you on the throne of Israel. Because of the Lord's eternal love for Israel, he has made you king to maintain justice and righteousness."

PRAYER:

Father, in the name of Jesus Christ, I praise You for You have delighted in me and enthroned me.

DAILY REFLECTION:

Take a moment to reflect on the Bible verse(s) for today and write your thoughts below:

December 6

BIBLE VERSE(S):

2 Chronicles 9:8 NIV

"Praise be to the Lord your God, who has delighted in you and placed you on his throne as king to rule for the Lord your God. Because of the love of your God for Israel and his desire to uphold them forever, he has made you king over them, to maintain justice and righteousness."

PRAYER:

Father, in the name of Jesus Christ, I thank You for delighting in me and placing me on a throne to rule for You, Lord.

DAILY REFLECTION:

Take a moment to reflect on the Bible verse(s) for today and write your thoughts below:

December 7

BIBLE VERSE(S):

Job 22:26 NIV

"Surely then you will find delight in the Almighty and will lift up your face to God."

PRAYER:

Father, in the name of Jesus Christ, today, I decree and declare that surely I will find delight in You and I will lift up my face to You, my God.

DAILY REFLECTION:

Take a moment to reflect on the Bible verse(s) for today and write your thoughts below:

December 8

BIBLE VERSE(S):

Psalm 1:2 NIV

"...but whose delight is in the law of the Lord, and who meditates on his law day and night. That person is like a tree planted by streams of water, which yields its fruit in season and whose leaf does not wither—whatever they do prospers."

PRAYER:

Father, in the name of Jesus Christ, I decree and declare that as I delight in Your law and meditate on it day and night, I become like a tree planted by streams of water, which yields its fruit in season and whose leaf does not wither so that whatever I do prospers.

DAILY REFLECTION:

Take a moment to reflect on the Bible verse(s) for today and write your thoughts below:

December 9

BIBLE VERSE(S):

Psalm 16:6 NIV

"The boundary lines have fallen for me in pleasant places; surely I have a delightful inheritance."

PRAYER:

Father, in the name of Jesus Christ, I decree and declare that the boundary lines have fallen for me in pleasant places and. surely, I have a delightful inheritance.

DAILY REFLECTION:

Take a moment to reflect on the Bible verse(s) for today and write your thoughts below:

December 10

BIBLE VERSE(S):

Psalm 18:19 NIV

"He brought me out into a spacious place; he rescued me because he delighted in me."

PRAYER:

Father, in the name of Jesus Christ, I thank You because You brought me out into a spacious place; You rescued me because You delighted in me.

DAILY REFLECTION:

Take a moment to reflect on the Bible verse(s) for today and write your thoughts below:

December 11

BIBLE VERSE(S):

Psalm 35:9 NIV

"Then my soul will rejoice in the Lord and delight in his salvation."

PRAYER:

Father, in the name of Jesus Christ, I decree and declare that my soul will rejoice in the Lord and delight in His salvation.

DAILY REFLECTION:

Take a moment to reflect on the Bible verse(s) for today and write your thoughts below:

December 12

BIBLE VERSE(S):

Psalm 35:27 NIV

"May those who delight in my vindication shout for joy and gladness; may they always say, 'The Lord be exalted, who delights in the well-being of his servant.'"

PRAYER:

Father, in the name of Jesus Christ, I decree and declare that those who delight in my vindication shall shout for joy and gladness. Thay shall say, 'The Lord be exalted, who delights in my well-being.'"

DAILY REFLECTION:

Take a moment to reflect on the Bible verse(s) for today and write your thoughts below:

December 13

BIBLE VERSE(S):

Psalm 37:3-4 NIV

"Trust in the Lord and do good; dwell in the land and enjoy safe pasture. Take delight in the Lord, and he will give you the desires of your heart."

PRAYER:

Father, in the name of Jesus Christ, I decree and declare that I trust in You Lord, and as I take delight in You, You will give me the desires of my heart.

DAILY REFLECTION:

Take a moment to reflect on the Bible verse(s) for today and write your thoughts below:

December 14

BIBLE VERSE(S):

Psalm 37:23 NIV

"The Lord makes firm the steps of the one who delights in him;"

PRAYER:

Father, in the name of Jesus Christ, I thank You for making my steps firm as I delight in You.

DAILY REFLECTION:

Take a moment to reflect on the Bible verse(s) for today and write your thoughts below:

December 15

BIBLE VERSE(S):

Psalm 43:4 NIV

"Then I will go to the altar of God, to God, my joy and my delight. I will praise you with the lyre, O God, my God."

PRAYER:

Father in the name of Jesus Christ, today, I go to the altar of God, to God, my joy and my delight. I will praise you, O God, my God.

DAILY REFLECTION:

Take a moment to reflect on the Bible verse(s) for today and write your thoughts below:

December 16

BIBLE VERSE(S):

Psalm 111:2 NIV

"Great are the works of the Lord; they are pondered by all who delight in them."

PRAYER:

Father, in the name of Jesus Christ, I decree and declare that great are Your works. I ponder on them and I delight in them.

DAILY REFLECTION:

Take a moment to reflect on the Bible verse(s) for today and write your thoughts below:

December 17

BIBLE VERSE(S):

Psalm 112:1 NIV

"Praise the Lord. Blessed are those who fear the Lord, who find great delight in his commands."

PRAYER:

Father, in the name of Jesus Christ, I praise You. I decree and declare that I am blessed for I fear the Lord and find great delight in His commands.

DAILY REFLECTION:

Take a moment to reflect on the Bible verse(s) for today and write your thoughts below:

BIBLE VERSE(S):

Psalm 119:16 NIV

"I delight in your decrees; I will not neglect your word."

PRAYER:

Father, in the name of Jesus Christ, I ask for the grace to delight in Your decrees and not neglect Your Word.

DAILY REFLECTION:

Take a moment to reflect on the Bible verse(s) for today and write your thoughts below:

December 19

BIBLE VERSE(S):

Psalm 119:24 NIV

"Your statutes are my delight; they are my counselors."

PRAYER:

Father, in the name of Jesus Christ, I thank You, for Your statutes are my delight and they are my counselors.

DAILY REFLECTION:

Take a moment to reflect on the Bible verse(s) for today and write your thoughts below:

December 20

BIBLE VERSE(S):

Psalm 119:35 NIV

"Direct me in the path of your commands, for there I find delight."

PRAYER:

Father, in the name of Jesus Christ, I ask that You direct me in the path of Your commands, for there I find delight.

DAILY REFLECTION:

Take a moment to reflect on the Bible verse(s) for today and write your thoughts below:

December 21

BIBLE VERSE(S):

Psalm 147:11 NIV

"...the Lord delights in those who fear him, who put their hope in his unfailing love."

PRAYER:

Father, in the name of Jesus Christ, I thank You for delighting in me, for I fear You and I put my hope in Your unfailing love.

DAILY REFLECTION:

Take a moment to reflect on the Bible verse(s) for today and write your thoughts below:

December 22

BIBLE VERSE(S):

Psalm 149:4 NIV

"For the Lord takes delight in his people; he crowns the humble with victory."

PRAYER:

Father, in the name of Jesus Christ, I thank You for delighting in me and crowning me with victory.

DAILY REFLECTION:

Take a moment to reflect on the Bible verse(s) for today and write your thoughts below:

December 23

BIBLE VERSE(S):

Isaiah 42:1 NIV

"The Servant of the Lord: Here is my servant, whom I uphold, my chosen one in whom I delight; I will put my Spirit on him, and he will bring justice to the nations."

PRAYER:

Father, in the name of Jesus Christ, I thank You for upholding me as Your chosen one in whom You delight and have put Your Spirit on.

DAILY REFLECTION:

Take a moment to reflect on the Bible verse(s) for today and write your thoughts below:

December 24

BIBLE VERSE(S):

Isaiah 62:4 NLT

"Never again will you be called 'The Forsaken City' or 'The Desolate Land.' Your new name will be 'The City of God's Delight' and 'The Bride of God,' for the Lord delights in you and will claim you as his bride."

PRAYER:

Father, in the name of Jesus Christ, I decree and declare that never again will I be called "The Forsaken City" or "The Desolate Land." My new name will be "The City of God's Delight" and "The Bride of God," for the Lord delights in me and will claim me as his bride.

DAILY REFLECTION:

Take a moment to reflect on the Bible verse(s) for today and write your thoughts below:

December 25

BIBLE VERSE(S):

Zephaniah 3:17 NLT

"For the Lord your God is living among you. He is a mighty savior. He will take delight in you with gladness. With his love, he will calm all your fears. He will rejoice over you with joyful songs."

PRAYER:

Father, in the name of Jesus Christ, I decree and declare that You are the Living God and a mighty savior. I thank You that You will take delight in me with gladness. With Your love, You will calm all my fears and rejoice over me with joyful songs.

DAILY REFLECTION:

Take a moment to reflect on the Bible verse(s) for today and write your thoughts below:

BIBLE VERSE(S):

Deuteronomy 30:9 AMP

"Then the Lord your God shall make you abundantly prosperous in everything that you do, in the offspring of your body and in the offspring of your cattle and in the produce of your land; for the Lord will again delight over you for good, just as He delighted over your fathers"

PRAYER:

Father, in the name of Jesus Christ, I thank You because You delight in prospering me and in making me abundantly prosperous in everything that I do. Today, I decree and declare that I shall receive more of Your blessings of prosperity.

DAILY REFLECTION:

Take a moment to reflect on the Bible verse(s) for today and write your thoughts below:

BIBLE VERSE(S):

Psalm 41:11 AMP

"By this I know that You favor and delight in me, Because my enemy does not shout in triumph over me."

PRAYER:

Father, in the name of Jesus Christ, I thank You because my enemy does not triumph over me, for You favor and delight in me.

DAILY REFLECTION:

Take a moment to reflect on the Bible verse(s) for today and write your thoughts below:

BIBLE VERSE(S):

Psalm 90:17 AMP

"And let the [gracious] favor of the Lord our God be on us; Confirm for us the work of our hands— Yes, confirm the work of our hands."

PRAYER:

Father, in the name of Jesus Christ, I decree and declare that the beauty, delightfulness, and favor of the Lord my God is upon me. Thank You, Lord, that You confirm and establish the work of my hands.

DAILY REFLECTION:

Take a moment to reflect on the Bible verse(s) for today and write your thoughts below:

December 29

BIBLE VERSE(S):

Psalm 94:19 AMP

"When my anxious thoughts multiply within me, Your comforts delight me.

PRAYER:

Father, in the name of Jesus Christ, I thank You because in the multitude of my thoughts, Your comforts cheer and delight my soul.

DAILY REFLECTION:

Take a moment to reflect on the Bible verse(s) for today and write your thoughts below:

December 30

BIBLE VERSE(S):

Psalm 111:2 NIV

"Great are the works of the Lord; they are pondered by all who delight in them."

PRAYER:

Father, in the name of Jesus Christ, I decree and declare that great are Your works. I will ponder on them for I delight in them.

DAILY REFLECTION:

Take a moment to reflect on the Bible verse(s) for today and write your thoughts below:

December 31

BIBLE VERSE(S):

Micah 7:18 AMP

"Who is a God like You, who forgives wickedness And passes over the rebellious acts of the remnant of His possession? He does not retain His anger forever, Because He [constantly] delights in mercy and lovingkindness."

PRAYER:

Father, in the name of Jesus Christ, I decree and declare that You are a God Who for forgives wickedness. You do not retain Your anger forever because You constantly delight in mercy and lovingkindness.

DAILY REFLECTION:

Take a moment to reflect on the Bible verse(s) for today and write your thoughts below:

Epilogue

Congratulations on praying and declaring the Word of God for a full year!

I trust that you have enjoyed the tremendous blessings of God in your life this year like never before and that you have developed a lifestyle of prayer inclusive of decreeing and declaring the biblical promises of God.

See you next year by God's grace. Let's continue to speak life and blessings based on Scripture, causing us to live a blessed and fabulous life in Christ Jesus.

God bless you abundantly.

Isioma

"Make your words good—you will be glad you did."
Proverbs 18:20-21, CEV

About the Author

Isioma Onuegwunwoke, J.D., MBA, LLM, is an accomplished contracts and risk management professional and an intentional living and self-care advocate with a passion for living a lifestyle of prayer based on the Word of God. She is the founder of *The Ladies Chill-Out* ('TLC"), a faith and prayer lifestyle booster, whose objective is to encourage women to prioritize self-care, foster a lifestyle of prayer, and positively impact and serve humanity, consequently living a blessed and fabulous life.

Milton Keynes UK
Ingram Content Group UK Ltd.
UKHW020655290424
441924UK00015B/865